Breaking Free

From the Street
to the Stage

First published by O Books, 2009
O Books is an imprint of John Hunt Publishing Ltd., The Bothy, Deershot Lodge, Park Lane, Ropley,
Hants, SO24 0BE, UK
office1@o-books.net
www.o-books.net

Distribution in:	South Africa
	Alternative Books
UK and Europe	altbook@peterhyde.co.za
Orca Book Services	Tel: 021 555 4027 Fax: 021 447 1430
orders@orcabookservices.co.uk	
Tel: 01202 665432 Fax: 01202 666219	Text copyright Christopher Lee Power 2008
Int. code (44)	
	Design: Stuart Davies
USA and Canada	Cover photograph: Jean-Pierre Magloire
NBN	
custserv@nbnbooks.com	ISBN: 978 1 84694 171 9
800 462 6420 Fax: 1 800 338 4550	
	All rights reserved. Except for brief quotations
Australia and New Zealand	in critical articles or reviews, no part of this
Brumby Books	book may be reproduced in any manner without
sales@brumbybooks.com.au	prior written permission from the publishers.
Tel: 61 . 1 5535 Fax: 61 3 9761 7095	
	The rights of Christopher Lee Power as author
Far East (offices in Singapore, Thailand,	have been asserted in accordance with the
Hong Kong, Taiwan)	Copyright, Designs and Patents Act 1988.
Pansing Distribution Pte Ltd	
kemal@pansing.com	A CIP catalogue record for this book is available
Tel: 65 6319 9939 Fax: 65 6462 5761	from the British Library.

Printed by CPI Antony Rowe, Chippenham, Wiltshire

Breaking Free

From the Street
to the Stage

Christopher Lee Power

BOOKS

Winchester, UK
Washington, USA

CONTENTS

Foreword

I have known Christopher for fifteen years. I first met him through a friend at my church - Chris Sanderson. Unfortunately Chris Sanderson was away so Christopher ended up spending the weekend with me. How many months that turned out to be I'm not sure but it was the commitment of an exciting and I know God given friendship between Christopher and myself.

Coming from a not dissimilar background to Christopher's with at least a portion of my own history very much like his and with having written stories and poems and acted and directed myself, I very soon discovered a rapport and empathy with Christopher, who became to me (and still is) the son I never had.

Life with him as my lodger was often great fun but not always plain sailing to say the least, particularly as we both have volatile temperaments. However God was in it and we are still as close today as ever.

His autobiography graphically indicates how Christopher has packed more into his 39 years than those who are more than double his age. From a very difficult and traumatic background and following a very Damascus Road and Christian Conversion, it has been a particular delight and encouragement for me to see how Christopher has grown and matured from the shy, insecure person he was to the giant he is today. Not only is he a Christian of whom I am sure God is proud but he is a talented actor and sings as well as a loving husband and father.

I am so grateful that I witnessed and was part of this amazing transition. I wish him well for the future and what a future I truly believe he has. **Richard Ford, Writer, Broadcaster.**

Thank You

I would like to thank everyone who has contributed to this book and particularly Richard Ford, Paul Attrell, David Bedrock, Jean-Pierre Magloire, and my wife and family for all their support.

CHAPTER 1

Roots

The hallway of the flat where I lived as a small child held a dark secret. One evening in 1972 when I was four years old my mum and dad went out to the local pub with their very good friends, Ronnie and Denise. As usual, our oldest sister Suzanne, who was aged ten, had to baby-sit us three younger children: my brother Carl, who was eight, my little sister Nicola, who was two and myself. An acquaintance of my dad and Ronnie from various street wars named David had argued with Ronnie in the pub that evening. Later that night he had arrived at Denise's house together with his wife, brandishing a knife and a gun, asking where my father and Ronnie had gone to.

My mum, not wanting to mention that they had returned to the flat to check on us, replied that she had no idea. David then put the gun to her head and said 'Someone will die tonight',

'Don't be silly, that gun isn't loaded,' replied my mum.

David became infuriated, pointed the gun to the ceiling and fired it. They both left, leaving my mum and Aunt Denise distressed though they quickly phoned the police. Meanwhile, my dad and Ronnie had come back to check on us all but as they made their way along the hallway to the flat they were confronted by their rivals in David's gang. It was here that an unpleasant fight broke out with screams and shouting, leaving my dad and Ronnie covered in blood. The sounds of sirens could be heard as the police rushed to the flat. It was not good: Ronnie was in a serious way and they were both taken to hospital. My mum soon arrived, only to be stopped by a WPC and escorted to a nearby police station. It was a stressful time for her and she had to wait an agonising hour, which must have seemed a lifetime, to hear news from the hospital. It was not long before the death of one of the two men was relayed back to the police station. What a relief when the news came that my dad was all right, apart from a leg wound. However it was devastating for Denise who had now become Ronnie's widow. Later that night mum was allowed back into the flat where another WPC had looked after us children. As mum entered the hallway the blood-stained handprints on the wall were all that were left as reminders of the awful situation. It would be another two days before the place could be finally cleaned, due to the necessary forensic examinations. Two people were eventually arrested and sent to prison. I now thank God that I never witnessed the blood stained walls. However, it did shock the local community that there had been a murder in Rock Ferry.

I have only a few memories of my past, but my mum, over the years, has shared and conveyed many of the facts. I was born Christopher Lee Power in 1968 and the family was, at that time, living in Oak and Eldon Gardens: a large concrete structure that dominated Birkenhead. I'm grateful that many years later it was demolished even if it had its fifteen minutes of fame on national television.

I was one of four children, although my mum had lost another five children in miscarriages. My dad, Christopher Michael Power, had been born in Liverpool along with his brother Johnny, who was a lot older. His mum, Christine Reilly, used to clean the old Victorian, sunken public toilets near Islington Road. These were happier times when I would visit my Nan while she was working and would be given pocket money and sweets. However, my Nan's past was not so clean because in her younger days she had experienced an attempted rape by a soldier in their home. Dad's memory of that awful night is still vivid. He remembers the screaming and, with his brother, ran downstairs only to find that the man had run away. He did, however, leave some evidence of being there in the form of his cap and this helped the police to trace him. My dad's father, Mr Power, was not so nice either, having beaten my Nan, which resulted in the loss of a baby. He then put my dad, as a small child, in an old tin bath full of dead mice. My Nan left him soon after this and she later remarried a man called Richie Philips. He was a grave digger, who also worked sometimes on a fruit and vegetable stall. One of my father's grandmothers had originated from Dublin in Ireland and, through her, our family has a gypsy heritage.

My mum, Evelyn, was born in Tranmere. She worked in Woolworth's on the hardware counter and always wanted to be a journalist, as well as a country and western singer. Her own mum was called Alice Joynson and she had her own shop in Price Street which was a general store. Her dad, Frank, worked at Cammell Lairds in Birkenhead.

Both of my parents have powerful stories to tell. They first met when my father was in prison on the Isle of Man. She had been visiting someone else with a friend. He was instantly attracted to her and tried to catch her attention and eventually succeeded. She started to write to him on a regular basis for a year and eventually, when he was released, they married on the Isle of Man. My mum was eighteen years old and he was twenty-two. He had been in and out of borstals and detention centres for much of his early life: over time he spent nearly eighteen years in and out of prison. My dad was a tough person and at one time he even took up boxing whilst in prison. I remember several occasions when he would go out and steal saleable things from cars to survive and look after the family. Dad has done his time and paid the price. Now in his seventieth year he has long given up that way of life and these days he enjoys his time with my mum listening to his old long playing records on an old player. My mum is extremely talented, both as a writer of poems and as a singer, and you only need to open the *Liverpool Echo* to read her marvellous poems. She gets excited at the thought that her poems could be printed in the *Liverpool Echo* at any time. I must make mention of dad's talent as a compere, which was his hobby during the weekend evenings and sometimes during the week. My dad was proud of his appearance on these nights. I would watch him when I was a teenager putting on his dinner suits ready to entertain the older generation in clubs and pubs, introducing the acts and even introducing my mother or myself if we were singing.

I don't remember living in Oak and Eldon Gardens flats because I was too young. My mum told me that a young boy had fallen from one of the verandas of the flats and this became a safety issue resulting in mum and dad moving to Rock Ferry. However, there was a problem over the rent being paid late and unfortunately mum and dad then had to find temporary accommodation above a taxi place. I do remember living above Abacus Taxis in Rock Ferry, which was where the murder of Ronnie took place. The upstairs flat had two bedrooms, a large living room and a small kitchen. Upstairs on the second floor was derelict and was never used. On one occasion I remember all of us sleeping in one bedroom for a while, whilst we had a room decorated. We had no toilet in the house and would have to make a journey downstairs, through a dark room to the yard, to an outside toilet. My sisters and brother, on many occasions, would line up and watch each other as we took turns to run across the yard to the toilet. There was no bathroom, so I was lifted up as a child and placed in the kitchen sink to have a bath and I still remember that this overlooked a very dark and bleak yard. We used to go across the road to mum's friend's house to have a bath on certain Sundays. This was very exciting as there was plenty of hot water from the taps and we were able to stretch out in what seemed like a very large bath to a small, five year old boy. One of my fondest memories of having a bath over the road was hearing the theme tune to *Black Beauty* blurting out while we washed ourselves. Our own flat gave us some good memories such as the Christmas tree being placed in the window for all to see, which was a glistening beacon to many. Years later, I was surprised just who remembered the proud large Christmas tree upstairs of Abacus Taxis. Christmas played a huge part in the Power family.

During the early 1970s Birkenhead was beginning to change. Money was being invested and new housing estates were emerging.

They say 'like father, like son' and that couldn't be closer to the truth. When I was still young and starting to experience what it meant to rebel, I witnessed my older brother Carl, who was eight or nine at the time, being attacked and hit with a bicycle chain, it was not a pleasant sight. He was a born fighter, like my father, and in years to come would gain a powerful reputation as one. As for me, I was timid until pushed to the limits since I was very ill as a child. I lacked co-ordination and suffered from a speech impediment and was therefore regularly in and out of hospital.

Stealing leaflets from milk floats at the age of four was the wrong choice for me and, because this was the path I took, it would eventually lead to my downfall as a person in later life. Meanwhile, our sister Suzanne had to grow up fast; she would regularly look after us and I enjoyed her company especially when mum and dad were out. We would make something to eat and rush into the large living room to watch a horror film.

In 1974 the family began a relocation to Conway Street in one of the long moving lorries. This was very exciting. I was six and life was beginning for me. When we arrived at the house it was a joy to find it had two toilets and a large garden. It was like being a royal. This was to be my parent's house until this day. Our time on top of Abacus Taxis was over, but on the opposite side of the road, near St Paul's Church, was a secret that only God knew about and which would not be revealed for another twenty-eight years.

CHAPTER 2

The Journey Begins

One of the advantages of moving to a newly-built estate was that all of the residents were new together and there was the opportunity to begin building relationships immediately. As with humans the world over, this was easier for some people than others. I started to attend Cathcart Street Primary School and having a school outside your own home was a real privilege, believe me. The estates had a youth club called St. Peter's, two churches, and many shops, including a funeral parlour. At the back of our estate, only a stone's throw away, was the - now near derelict - Oak and Eldon Gardens, a reminder of where life for me began, but it had only a few residents left. It was not long before the entire block of flats was empty and this was good news for the youths on our estate. Bonfire night was a few months away and the traditions relied on finding an old derelict building and to stockpile some wood that would be needed for bonfire night. I remember joining the youths as they started to pull off doors from the empty flats. Watching these doors being thrown out of flats, on to the grass, ready for the fifth of November was a spectacular sight. It was also an exciting time for 'Guy Fawking', a tradition in the UK. I remember rumbling around drawers in our house hoping to find an old pair of trousers, jumper and a wig. I then stuffed the legs of the trousers with newspaper and the same with the jumper and created something that resembled a ventriloquist doll. The nights leading up to bonfire night, groups of youths would claim their territory outside a shop or pub and ask as many people as they could for money. 'A penny for the Guy,' was the usual line to say. Occasionally you would find that your 'Guy Falk' would come under attack from drunken revelers looking for a laugh. Looking back, I made a lot of money.

Gang warfare was very prominent during the seventies and, although it would be another five years before I joined a well-known gang, this would be a taster.

The gangs based in each estate would choose a name, something associated to their street or where they lived, almost tribal somehow. For example, if you lived in Bidston then you would call yourselves the Bidston gang. As fires started to light up the night sky, the children and adolescents together would build barricades and attack other youths with bottles and stones. Unfortunately for me, I was often in the firing line and once was hit in the eye with a bolt. This was very painful and I ran home with blood rushing down my face. I needed stitches from the casualty department at the nearest hospital. However, it didn't stop me from entering into more conflicts. In fact I was enjoying this kind of life. I was becoming rebellious. This was the start of my downfall and, after leaving Cathcart Street School and moving into Conway Middle School, I began to be a bully amongst my peers.

School was somehow never quite as exciting after my brother Carl left for secondary school, so I decide to play truant on a regular basis. I was taken to see a doctor who, from the result of a blood test, decided that I was hyperactive and, additionally, had speech difficulties, needing a few operations on my adenoids and teeth. I spent a few months in Thingwall Hospital, which also had children that I knew from our estate, so this was not such a bad time for me. Most of the children had problems either with asthma or epilepsy, but I was just hyperactive and hated school. At the same time, social services decided that I would have to be sent to the adjacent special school, where the only good thing was that you went home at the weekends and arrived back on a Sunday evening to banana sandwiches. I have a few memories of this time, including an attempt to run away, only to be caught and returned.

Not too far away from the hospital was a valley with a stream and woods. After school, a group of us would make our way to the valley and break into a shed where the gardener kept his tools. Once inside we would take the large saw and stroll into the woods to saw wood. I remember the excitement of trying to saw through large logs. There was also the aroma of leaves and a kind of woody smell that would linger in the air. Even now, if I am walking through a park, this aroma still reminds me of the valley, not forgetting the sound of the stream and its trickling water. At night, as one can imagine, it was dark and I used to play a game, which was to make my way to the girl's dormitory without any one seeing me - good fun if you don't get caught. I also remember building a stage and performing for the parents on one occasion. The acorn of acting had been planted but it began to germinate in rebellious ways. I enjoyed the limelight and applause but was getting it from my friends for the wrong reasons. It was for rebelling, stealing and committing minor crimes. One night I was taken under a hospital bed and sexually abused by an older boy. This was the first of several incidents of similar abuse and the thought of it sometimes fuels anger within me, as I will later mention.

My parents didn't want me to be in hospital any more; it was too much for them. They loved me and one night my dad arrived in his car and took me back home, unaware of my abuse. Mum and dad found themselves fighting with the authorities regarding my being taken out of hospital without the hospital's permission. God must have had His hand on us as a family, because eventually we won and I went back to school, putting Thingwall Hospital firmly at the back of my mind.

Another bonfire night had approached only to be ruined this time, not by youths fighting, but by an explosion. Someone had placed a gas cylinder on a fire which then exploded and blew out windows. Finally, in 1979, Oak and Eldon Gardens would end its days by being demolished by dynamite. The day before the event, our dog, Scamp, had gone missing. Suzanne, my sister, had brought Scamp home as a young pup when she was 15 years old. I had given up all hope and went for a walk. I decided to walk past the flats and suddenly noticed a workman bringing out this black dog. It was our dog. I started to choke up and realised that she must have wandered into the flats the previous night.

On the day of the demolition the estate residents were asked to evacuate from the estate and make our way towards Birkenhead Docks for safety. We were given special passes to show when we were allowed back home. This was to prevent loiterers. TV and newspaper reporters pointed their cameras to get a good view and then came the moment we were all waiting for. A siren was sounded before Oak and Eldon Gardens became a pile of rubble. There was dust everywhere. This was the end of an era for Oak and Eldon Gardens, but unfortunately the beginning of my downfall.

I had been invited to stay with my uncle John in Liverpool. They lived on the first floor of a maisonette. One night, whilst in my cousin's bedroom, I heard my Uncle, who had arrived home late drunk, arguing with his friend. It was very heated and concerned me. I found it difficult and became rather frightened. The next morning I made a decision to sneak out of the house and, with the money I had left in my pocket, made my way on a Liverpool bus to catch the Mersey Ferry across to Birkenhead. My uncle and cousins, at this time, were unaware of my departure. This was the day that would change my life. As I approached the front door I noticed the glass had been broken. My cousin Joanne opened the door, all was not as it seemed. My mum was lying on the settee but no dad. Joanne started to explain to me what had happened. Hearing that my dad had been locked up by the police upset me and I started to fill up, resulting in my crying and running away from the house. Joanne came after me and placed her arms around me in the hope of bringing some comfort. As the day progressed, it became very clear regarding the difficult situation I had come home to.

Now, one thing I have to say about my dad - although I love

him - is that once he had a drink and allowed himself to become intoxicated he was a different man. His temper was terrible and not pleasant. What happened next shocked me and the memory has remained with me even to this day. Mum and dad had gone out for a meal and when they arrived home the police knocked at the door. Unaware that there had been a robbery in the area and the police were making enquiries, my dad started to argue with the police. He was trying to protect his home. The police tried to restrain him. My mum watched in horror as the police restrained him in the police car. A few days later Nicola and Suzanne visited my dad in hospital with my mum. My mum also made a statement about what had gone on. My dad alleged that he was stripped naked and beaten with batons. My sister could not believe it when she visited him. In her words he was 'unrecognisable'. The newspapers reported that he had been charged with assault on thirteen police officers. This was a painful memory for me and fuelled my anger, at what I believed was an injustice, to the point of hating most people in authority. After a few weeks of recovering, dad finally came home but his anger would remain with him for a long time.

It was around this time that I used to visit a shop on Conway Street, until one afternoon a man, who I had grown to trust, took advantage of that trust by taking me to the back of the shop and sexually abusing me. He started touching my body and because I was vulnerable, like a lot of children I was searching for attention and affection, I did not stop him. However, I knew that this did not seem right and felt ashamed to tell anyone, so I didn't share it, thinking that it was my fault. It took me a long time to realise that I was a victim. This man had lured me into his business, groomed me and built up my trust only to destroy it with the abuse. Looking back, who is to say that this man didn't have a paedophile ring he knew about? I could have been killed.

The abuse didn't stop here. I found myself - on one occasion, not far from home - being taken off the street, into a garage, by two women, who I knew from the area. As one kept lookout, the other woman had unprotected sex with me. I was still only about eleven. These ladies were breaking the law as well as the other man. The other lady also wanted sex but I could not. As the months went on, the abuse became more frequent. One man, not far from my home, took me and abused me. I blamed myself and thought that I could have run away; after all, I participated in the acts. Around this time, I was now, not only angry with the police and myself for the abuse, but I was also searching for identity.

This was also a time of change for me regarding friendship. I had started to associate with a group of young people who would eventually become a notorious gang in the eighties. As a family, we tried to move on from the traumas that had affected our lives. Carl, Suzanne, Nicola and I all had one thing in common: we didn't really like school. Our dad was strict and discipline was instilled in us which, in the long run was beneficial. I remember on Sundays, my dad would write a list of things to do before we could go out and they had to be done. However, the family would enjoy a traditional game of Monopoly on most occasions. Christmas, as usual, was great fun and my dad would put the Christmas decorations up before most people, but I didn't mind as it was an exciting time for our family. My mum loved to dress our home and put up the Christmas lights. My sister Nicola and I would often walk around the shops along Grange Road looking at toys during the Christmas period: which was a tradition for us both. On a Sunday morning my brother and sisters and I would often run down to Charles Thompson Mission to attend the morning service. At the end we looked forward with great anticipation to be given a ticket which we could redeem on Thursday evenings and would each get a toy, a bun, and a packet of crisps after the service.

CHAPTER 3

It's an Emu

Conway Street was a long road and, not only did you gain access to our house from the street but my next school was in walking distance of the house. Conway Middle School was a very old building and had a history; built at the turn of the 20th Century, it still had 'BOYS' and 'GIRLS' engraved into its brickwork at the entrances. The desks had ink-wells set into the tops and many other original features, such as the wooden doors and windows and stone floor. Mr. Powell was the headmaster and Mr. Shardlow was my teacher. Teachers would play a very important part in my life and I'm not just talking about the formal education they provided. I hated most of them and even went out of my way to annoy them, with the exception of Mr. Shardlow of whom I was very fond. After all, it was he who introduced me to acting, not knowing how it would change my life in later years. 'Singing Together' was a favourite lesson of mine. We would all sit around something that looked like a wooden radiator and listen to a radio programme which taught us how to use musical instruments. At the end of one large classroom was a door that reminded me of *The Lion, the Witch, and the Wardrobe*. When you entered through this large oak door you found yourself in an old auditorium. This was where we watched television programmes like *Watch* (part of the BBC's TV for Schools output). Sometimes we would also perform on the little stage.

I soon befriended a few people from Conway and the surrounding schools. These would later become the core group of the gang that I would eventually be a part of. Mark was one such good friend of mine and we would also meet up occasionally after school. However, for us, like many children promising to remain friends and even attend the same school, life can throw up spontaneous changes. We had both decided to attend Rock Ferry High School when we left Conway Middle School but, on the day that our requests had to be handed in, a fight broke out between us. During playtime that day, I made my way to the classroom without anyone knowing and found the paperwork on the teacher's desk. I changed my entry from Rock Ferry School to the Birkenhead Institute School for Boys, not realising how this would be used for good in the near future.

I had started to steal again and I can clearly remember the time that I stole some tea towels and sold them for five crispy pound notes and took Steven, another good friend, to see *Grease* at the ABC Cinema. My mother wasn't pleased. The ABC was what we, at the time, considered to be a large cinema. In the foyer was a long counter selling sweets. Unlike today, when most of the confectionary is sold in large bags and the drinks are available in paper cups at a premium price, you could buy a single mars bar, polo mints or other sweets at the counter. Once inside, you were shown to your seat by a lady with a torch and there were three areas of seating including a balcony. Sometimes, when we could not afford our own tickets, a group of us would scrape together enough money to pay to get one person in and then the rest of us would wait around by the back door until we were let in by our friend, through the exit door.

At Conway Middle School there was a teacher called Mr. Speed, which was ironic because he had a bad leg and would hobble wherever he went. He took us, once, for a craft class and when he left the room I chatted to the other children and decided to go on strike, not knowing that the entire class would become cowards. When asked why I was not participating I replied, 'I am on strike Sir.'

He was not amused and dragged me downstairs to the headmaster's study. With no excuses for my behaviour, the head used a slipper on me and sent me straight back to class. Mr. Powell was someone with whom, many years later, I was to come into contact with, but for a quite different reasons and in an unusual way. I was rapidly becoming a very rebellious person. When Christmas approached Mr. Shardlow had cast me as 'the boy who goes to buy Scrooge a huge turkey' in A *Christmas Carol*. However, some of us couldn't bring ourselves to take it seriously because Bob Cratchit (played by Gary, a dear friend of mine) was given the next best thing we could find for a turkey. It was an emu. Nevertheless, the play was a success and inspired me to continue in an artistic way.

Time at Conway Middle School was drawing to a close, but not before our class had one final mission. Right at the top of our school was a blue tower and, legend had it that, a ghost of a boy dressed in blue walked the corridors. Some of us decided to check out the story for ourselves. Climbing the spiral staircase prompted my imagination to go wild. At the top, there was a small flat with a bathroom that overlooked the rooftop. I decided to go into the bathroom and closed the door, only to find that as I tried to get back out the door would not open. I became frightened and shouted for help. Help was summoned and Mr. Shardlow came to my aid. When I told him that the door was jammed he replied, 'Pull the handle.' I gave the handle a sharp pull, as I had a lot of strength, and as I stepped back the handle was now in my hand and the door remained firmly stuck. Eventually, some brute force solved the problem and, with a karate kick from Mr. Shardlow, the door was finally opened. It was not long before I was due to go into the final stage of my education... or so I thought.

CHAPTER 4

Experiments

The moment had arrived and it was time for me to enter the final hurdle of my education. I attended Birkenhead Institute and, with my school grant, bought my first blazer and badge. We weren't wealthy in the eighties. I remember on many occasions my mum borrowing a few pound notes from a neighbour to buy the basics, such as bread, potatoes and butter. As a family, I remember we would toast bread on an old electric fire which became a tradition in our household even if it did take a long time. We enjoyed the taste a lot better than a conventional grill.

At the back of our house, the other youths on the estate would play something called 'Jumping the wall.' Basically, you would stand on a wall and jump across an entry to the other side. Around the back of our house was a mortuary. Many of the youths played on the roof of the mortuary until, on one occasion, one of the youths, called Jerry, kicked the door open of this building, revealing a dead body. It was not a pleasant sight. Most of the youths from our estate would stay out late most nights playing hide and seek or just talking for hours.

At the back of the estate, families started to leave their homes, as their houses were to be demolished ready for regeneration. I was curious though: why were John and David locking themselves in the outside toilet? I later discovered that they were sniffing solvents. It wasn't long before I started experimenting with glue. Unfortunately, drug abuse took over for the next seven years of my life.

I had departed from the gang I associated with to join a group from one of the most rundown areas. Across the road was an old bakery where I had been stealing bread from a year or so back. It had been demolished and became our drug den. For many months at least four of us would congregate and sniff glue for most of the day. People could always tell because we would have glue all over us and a glazed look. Polo mints were a trick of the trade and were used to disguise our breath.

I used to be a member of St. Peter's Youth Club in the seventies and discos were very popular at this youth club. There was nothing I enjoyed more than attending these nights out. I was a show off! I would walk onto the dance floor like John Travolta from *Saturday Night Fever*. Around Birkenhead, during this time, there were many derelict places, such as railway stations and garages, all used as dens to sniff glue.

Stealing was an everyday thing for me during this time. I became addicted to sniffing glue and as a result, I stole to feed my addiction. I also stole the communion wine from a local church and got drunk on it. I had no thought about God at this point.

There were, however, consequences to sniffing glue: I was becoming a recluse and locking myself away in the bedroom, spending hours away from the family. Once my dad found out that I had been sniffing glue, he punished me and I had to stay in for many days. It took time to stop the solvents but finally the glue sniffing stopped. I remember one incident when a gang of youths shouted, 'Glue sniffer,' which was hurtful, but after much thought I decided that I had to start afresh with my life. I finally joined the group of young people that I had built up a relationship with in my local area. It was an exciting time for me. I became a member of a gang called 'The Priests.' I remember trying to sell four pairs of jeans that I had stolen from a shop but, unfortunately for me, I was caught by CID and charged. There was even one occasion when someone broke into a fruit shop, only to foolishly leave a trail of bananas skins behind them.

We would meet at a café on Conway Street and spend hours sitting around the Space Invaders machine. We wanted to establish ourselves, but this would take more than sitting in a café or on the long wall outside. We used to hang out at another café called Pete's, which had a pinball machine and a pool table, but our favourite treat here was a bacon sandwich with a cup of tea. The ska bands; *Madness, The Specials* and *The Jam* dominated the charts and mods, trogs and punks started to emerge in Birkenhead. The mods would park their scooters outside the Birkenhead Market and the trogs would be outside Skeleton's record shop opposite Beattie's department store.

On the corner of Conway Street was a car accessory shop and, over many weeks, 'The Priests' would buy tins of spray paint and head towards Birkenhead Park to spray our names in big bold letters. The park was not just for young kids to play ball games in or older people to walk their dogs; it was also a major social area for teenage boys and girls. It was the place where we would drink our stolen, or otherwise illicitly-obtained, Merrydown cider (a popular drink for many and especially for those who were underage!) As bonfire night approached once more, 'The Priests' would buy a load of fireworks, put them in bottles and then light them. It was very much a boy's thing, watching these bottles explode. I could not drive at this time but some other gang members could and were very good. I remember some of them stealing cars and getting caught by the police. One of the games most frequently played by the gang was 'British Bulldogs,' where you divide into teams and one team would hide in a certain area waiting to be rooted out by the other team. When you were caught you had to stay in a certain area guarded by the other members. On many occasions this game was played in and amongst flats and buildings ready for demolition, such as a school called St Hughes in Oxton. Some of my friends use to attend this school until it was closed down.

St. Peter's Youth Club was where we mostly hung out in the evenings. Unfortunately, it got torched by some members of a rival gang and so we descended on Charing Cross Youth Club. It had the nickname of 'The Dolly.' The year was 1981 and this place was much more exciting: it had pool and table tennis tables and a great café run by a lady called Margaret and a, hitherto unknown, youth worker called Stuart Melling, who was thirty one years old and had come from Wigan. He was to become an important person in my life. I was an attention seeker, wanting approval and acceptance. 'The Priests' too were collectively much the same and we had started making a name for ourselves at 'The Dolly.' Stuart had taken us in a minibus, on one occasion, to Birkenhead Park to informally chat to us before we could join the youth club. This was his way of saying, 'I don't mind you coming in to the club but don't mess me around'.

The eighties were an exciting time. *Madness* posters dominated our bedroom walls and, as a gang, we needed an identity. We wanted the other gangs to know who we were, not just by name but also by the way we dressed. We had green parka jackets, skinhead haircuts and combat boots. 'The Priests' were becoming even more popular in the area. More young people wanted to join. Sometimes, myself and one of the gang members, called Paul would go off together to have a cigarette and steal lead from derelict buildings. It was on such an occasion that I was first caught by the police and charged with theft and criminal damage. My dad wasn't at all pleased, having to drive to the police station and bail me out of the cells. This rapidly became an all too frequent occurrence. I started to enjoy the prestige of being a criminal and the attention it brought. The name Christopher Power was becoming a popular one, heard on the streets of Birkenhead by the gangs if not by the authorities. However, deep inside me was still the need to be loved and accepted.

CHAPTER 5

Bonding

At 'The Dolly' youth club, Stuart had noticed my energetic and aggressive nature, which was causing problems. He asked me to leave the club once and wanted to ban me. As already mentioned, I had problems with anyone in authority and I picked up a chair, threatening to break one of the windows. Stuart softened his approach, empathising with me, which became a defining moment for both of us. A bond between us started to emerge.

A similar bond had occurred previously at a local after-school play scheme many years before. Paul and his brothers - all good friends of mine - used to attend the play scheme at the back of the youth club. Inside was a favourite room of ours which was a tool room and housed hundreds of tools, some of which would, at times, be stolen, never to be seen again. The play scheme leader, Peter Brandrick, was about twenty-one years old and new to youth work. He was also a diabetic, so his blood sugar levels would at times be low. One day I climbed up onto the roof of the play scheme building and idly lobbed some stones at his assistant's car. I was soon spotted, immediately banned and spent the next few weeks waiting patiently outside, trying to catch Peter's attention in the hope of being allowed back in, but every time I was turned down. However, one day Peter invited Paul to accompany him during a visit to WH Smiths to get some materials and I was asked to go along too, which for me seemed like a miracle. I had to prove to him that I could be well-behaved - at least some of the time. I think this convinced him that I wasn't totally bad and he allowed me back in. That night, Peter (who was a great artist,) invited me to the local Methodist church to watch him paint the nativity backdrop. From that moment on, it was great fun being at that play scheme. He was also to become a good friend to 'The Priests' later on. Peter was someone you could really talk to when you found yourself in trouble and he even recorded a song, which I sang with 'The Priests,' called 'Seven Little Girls, Sitting in the Backseats,' though our version was never as popular as the Paul Evans original (or even the 1990 Timmy Mallett recording!) I remember travelling to Sandy Beach in Anglesey with 'The Priests' and Peter Brandrick. It was an exciting time for us as a group. We were young, away from our parents and free to break rules such as drinking cider every night, which did not please Peter, who was - as mentioned earlier - a diabetic. The last thing he needed was a group of youths, drinking and shouting abuse at some bikers outside a pub. Apart from the not-so-good dinners that had been cooked for us by another youth worker called Ma Baker we had fun.

Back at 'The Dolly,' Stuart Melling was building relationships with the gang. I was very possessive of Stuart and this was seen in the way I would, on most occasions, get his attention. If Stuart didn't take any notice I would make it known either by walking off or dominating the conversation. One evening, someone at the club mentioned that the Beechcroft Theatre on nearby Whetstone Lane, which was run by a lady called Mary Oston, was running a drama workshop. I decided to attend one evening and see if I could get involved. I didn't know much about acting, but it seemed like a fun thing to do and so it proved to be.

After leaving the drama workshop that night I visited an arcade called 'The Silver Strike,' hoping to meet with some of the gang. It had become an occasional meeting place for lots of young people, often packed on Saturday nights and some time later it would become my second home for many years. Some of my money got stuck in one the machines and I became annoyed. The attendants noticed me trying to rock the slot machine and asked me to leave: I got angry and, on my way out, kicked a window through in retaliation. Once outside, I quickly ran into a pub a short distance away to hide. In an attempt to shield me, some of the actors from the Beechcroft stood up when the staff from the 'Strike' came in after me. Despite their efforts, I was caught and handed over to the police, arrested and charged with criminal damage. The courts gave me another fine and a supervision order. Once again my dad was far from pleased.

I had enjoyed all of the attention I got from 'The Priests,' which they gave me regarding going to court.

The acting bug started to excite me at this time in my life. I was nearly a teenager and Stuart had started to take more of an interest in my life, even coming to a juvenile court in Wallasey to support me. Occasionally, I would improvise situations with Stuart at the youth club, keeping a straight face as I told an out-and-out lie, trying to fool the other lads into believing our stories. This was good fun and many were there times that the others would fall for our tales.

During the eighties, several local gangs started to emerge with such names as 'Forecast,' 'Oxton' and 'Ford Estate.' Stuart the youth worker once said that he had seen a title of a book called 'Let the flowers grow' and remembered something from the book. Stuart paraphrased it like this:

'Birkenhead was like a field and flowers needed space to grow with the sun and rain. However, when there were too many flowers dominating the space they would compete against each other.'

He went on to tell me that, at one time, young people had plenty of jobs to go to. For example, there was a thriving ship building industry at the Cammell Laird yard adjacent to Birkenhead Docks. Most families in the area would have at least one relative who worked there. It gave them many occupations and self respect and an identity. However, Stuart felt that this had changed and many young people during this period went on to the dole as soon as they left school. Feeling despair and hopelessness, with no work prospects, they found comfort with each other and this became the accepted view of how the gangs emerged.

Another question that could be asked is: why do people join gangs? For me, personally, I wanted respect, status, power, money and a sense of belonging. Others had come from good homes, but wanted the excitement. There were also those who had been excluded from school, suffered family break-ups, neglect and poverty. For them, being in a gang was substitute family. 'The Priests' certainly started off as a group of friends who trusted, supported and protected each other. I think as other gangs emerged it became one of survival. I feel that although I don't condone violence, I do believe that one of the major difference between the 'The Priests' and today's gangs is technology. There is easy access to information on the internet, easy access to guns, weapons and mobile phones, which contribute to gangs being more organising. With *YouTube* I think (and it is a personal opinion) that young people have been desensitised to violence such as happy slapping (a term used to describe a situation that may involve fighting or being physically assaulted being filmed on a mobile). Young people today have more access to drugs and weapons. It seems to have become a fashionable status symbol to have a gun. In the eighties, the only guns that we had were legal and bought from a model shop. These were pellet guns and used for fun in the park or at Birkenhead Docks. Occasionally these pellet guns would be misused. I remember being shot in the head by a pellet gun and, to this day, I don't know if it was an accident. It did hurt and left a huge bump on my forehead. Thus, 'The Priests' needed to claim their title and territory as the best. This would take time, and a lot of preparatory groundwork had to be done.

CHAPTER 6

Boys' School

Birkenhead Institute was my final school and an all boys' school. It had some old traditions and I was introduced to a strict regime of detention, the cane and hard work. Some of the teachers, including the deputy headmaster, Mr Malcolm, would walk through the corridors with their black gowns, radiating their authoritative presence. Birkenhead Institute was built in an 'H' kind of shape and, as you walked through the corridors (which were mostly glass) and down or up the stairwells, history would be staring you in the face. The bricks were dark and shiny and, as you entered the workshops (such as the science labs,) you could not but notice the old, long desks with the gas taps in the middle. On many occasions, I would hear stories of pupils lighting the gas taps for fun.

The school had a large library called 'The Wilfred Owen Library,' named after the First World War poet. There was, however, a new building, called the 'Sixth Form Block.' It was here that you would find the 'Prefects;' those pupils who had decided to stay on after the four years were up. The Prefects would walk around the school corridors, with their little badges on and suits, letting the younger pupils know that they had a certain authority and if you did anything wrong they could take you by the arm and frog-march you to a headmaster's office. If you weren't in the sixth form, but showed that you had worked diligently and could be trusted, you could possibly be in line for a monitor's job with a yellow or red shield and tasks such as monitoring corridors. To my knowledge, I think Mr. Morris (better known to the pupils as 'Nogger,') had a lot to do with the sixth form block. Other teachers that I remember having nick names, for whatever reason, were; 'Taffy,' a French teacher; 'The

Penguin,' because of his walk. Mr. Maxim, the new deputy head after Mr. Malcolm had left, would walk around the class using his enormous size to instill fear into his students and making pronouncements like, 'As far as I'm concerned, the next person to get it wrong will feel the end of my Cane.' These are only a few of the teachers who taught at the school.

Psychology has, over the years, been used in certain organisations and varies in its many forms, but one of the ways that psychology - in my opinion - is used is with the employment of privileges, rewards, ranks and different hats to determine what groups you are in. If there are any competitions, this can be an incentive to win something or to determine status. At Birkenhead Institute we had, what were called, 'Houses,' represented by coloured ties and named after people who had attended the school. These were Stitt, Davis, Atkins, Westminster, Cohen and Tate (which was my house).

I began to become more aggressive towards certain teachers. This was largely due to my uncontrollable anger and, when aggravated, I would turn into a frightened, cornered animal and wouldn't think twice about picking up a chair or a knife. It was a case of a misplaced defensive attitude and I rounded aggressively on my 'tormentors.' Whilst in the playground one day, I noticed a young black boy looking through a telescope and asked him what he was doing. He replied, 'Looking at the gravestones,' indicating towards a nearby cemetery.

His name was Jean-Pierre Magloire and it marked the start of a friendship that would last right up to the present. In my opinion, compared with most of my, then, current friends, Jean-Pierre seemed very educated and knew things that impressed me. We chatted, enjoyed many of the same subjects, hung out and everyday our friendship grew. Every afternoon he would go into the school hall and play the piano. Being blind in one eye never stopped him from achieving his goals and he had been given special permission to practise during break times. There were only a few times, during the three years at Birkenhead Institute, that we fell out with one another. There were few occasions that we didn't sit at adjacent desks, but one of these times was in an English class with a female teacher. Instead, he was sitting directly behind me and I was very annoyed and envious because he had made a decision to sit with Nick Williams. I turned around and shouted at him, accidentally hitting him with my elbow. He was upset at this and hit me back. I picked up a chair and threw it across the room. Mr. Hume, a nice teacher from Scotland, came into the classroom and our teacher asked if I would care to repeat my actions, thinking that she had regained control and that I would not attempt a stunt like that in front of a male teacher. How wrong she was. I threw another chair and Mr Hume summoned me outside and put me on detention.

This aggression became very addictive and I found myself fighting, spitting at and chasing the teachers. Sometimes I would pick fights in the corridor with two or three teachers to get attention, but also part of me had hatred to certain authorities. It was due to the incident that happened with my dad all those years ago, when he was arrested by the police, which I still thought about. On one such occasion, Mr. Moony, a new teacher had remonstrated against me in front of the class for not participating in the work that had been given to us. Mr Moony started walking towards me and, as he got closer to ask me to leave the class, I took one look at him and swore at him. He was not amused and, grabbed my blazer, lifting me out of the chair. Jean-Pierre saw my eyebrows rise up and indicated to another friend that this gesture spelt trouble. I became incensed with rage against Mr. Moony and lashed out at him with my fist, then grabbed the green bin, attempting to put it over his head. It wasn't long before we were both in the corridor with two other teachers, who had come from the nearby classrooms, and soon we were all wrestling with each other. Eventually another teacher called 'The Oggy,' who was from Liverpool, shouted at the other teachers to stop. He was very good at defusing the situation and we both went off to the school hall so that I could calm down. The outcome of this incident resulted in my being caned.

I was, on other occasions, given detentions and suspended. Through it all, Jean-Pierre and I still remained friends. I would regularly bunk off school, smoke under the school stage and get drunk. My dad had a bar at home and, one time, I drank brandy before school and arrived there drunk out of control and ended up performing such drunken antics as jumping on the school stage curtains and flicking peas at people during lunch in the dining hall.

There was another boy called Richard, who was also a good friend. He and I decided to start a gang at school. During break time we would try and get through the corridors without being seen, this was great fun. One time, 'Batty,' a small, slim boy, tried to get through one of the small windows and I couldn't stop laughing because we knew a teacher was coming down the hallway. 'Batty' was fortunate because he got out in time and made his way to the playground. The boys at the school also found out that I was a member of 'The Priests' gang and some of the violence from outside began to spill over into school, as rival gangs started to fight with each other. I was nearly knocked out by one gang on the corridor. Despite the fact that in my earlier schools I had been a bully, I began to find that I was starting to be bullied whilst at school. The image that I was trying to portray meant that the situation couldn't be allowed to continue, so one day I approached one of my bullies and attacked him. He never bullied me again.

Outside of school I continued to steal, as I was addicted to gambling and enjoyed the power of having money, but I was arrested and sent to an attendance centre each Saturday, depriving me of being with my friends, which was a terrible punishment to me. It consisted of a highly regimented two hours. First we would all line up and then we were taken off to a large hall where we did foot drill. As punishments went, marching seemed quite good fun. Following this, we were made to scrub the floors of the building until they were gleaming. The last hour was exercise with a tough workout in the sports hall. My criminal record was fast expanding and I spent many hours in attendance centres.

I blame myself for lack of education because I was too involved with 'The Priests,' fighting and having fun. However, looking back, I do wish that some of the teachers had been bold enough to take me aside and support me in education and, unfortunately, we didn't have drama at the institute – one of the few things that I was really interested in and skilled at.

My brother Carl, who is four years older than me, was only there for one year before he left. I tried to be careful this time, so that I didn't use his reputation to help me be successful at school, wanting to be recognised as an individual in my own right.

Christmas time would be an exciting and special time for Jean-Pierre and me. We enjoyed the autumn months. I can still remember the many snowball fights we had with the other boys and the odd teacher. In the playground, boys' trouser pockets were used as market stores and much business would go on right under the noses of the teachers. The boys with pocket money would go to the nearby shop and buy sweets, then sell them at much higher prices, making huge profits. You always knew when a fight would be starting because boys would chant this silly tune: 'Ere r err e-r err.' The same ritual silly tune would be chanted so many times a week.

Without any formal drama, the place I felt most at home during school hours was on the stage with Jean-Pierre, either singing to his favourite Gilbert and Sullivan songs, as he belted them out on the piano keys, or trying to learn Beethoven's *Moonlight Sonata*, which he painstakingly taught me as the months went on. Art classes were interesting: as usual we would sit together painting and talking, but also listening to the teacher called 'The Devil,' because of his little beard. He would regularly shout at two boys called Peter and Kelly at the top of his voice. My name too was frequently mentioned at school and so now I had a reputation to keep up amidst competition.

CHAPTER 7

Gangs of Birkenhead

'The Priests' didn't like those people who knew who we were and where we hung out. Most people would be frightened to walk past the long wall on Conway Street, where 'The Priests' would sit and chat, making us feel powerful. I suppose they were afraid of being attacked. Every so often, the hairdressers on that street would have a field day, shaving off hair to give us our trademark skinhead look. One by one, we would walk out looking like new army recruits. The violent and destructive army-like style of living played a huge part in our growth as a gang. We would, for example, have an aim to do something daring, such as finding a row of old derelict houses and seeing how fast we could get through the walls that connected each building. Some of us would use set tools; carelessly wielding sledgehammers and others would take out one brick at a time in a more deliberate and careful attempt.

Abseiling down from certain rooftops was a fun pastime and, looking back, I'm surprised that no one was killed or even seriously injured. We were not thinking about the dangers at that moment. We were very fit and had a lot of energy to expend. The oldest members (Tom, Gary and Tony) had started to go to night-clubs, leaving those of us who were underage to find our own enjoyment, which mostly, during those times, consisted of house parties. Being underage didn't always stop us from going to pubs or clubs, either because we looked big and old enough, or because we could use intimidation, but house parties were better: lots of girls and drink, and the new invention of the decade – the video player. I remember the first one in our home, which came complete with a remote control connected to the video with a cable and with a button that made a loud clunking noise when pressed making the top loader spring up.

It became quite apparent that sex, alcohol and stealing would be part of my lifestyle for some time.

'The Priests' heard, through word of mouth, that one of the other gangs wanted to meet us in Birkenhead Park – and it wasn't for a picnic! War had broken out amongst the groups, who were each trying to protect (and if possible enlarge) their territories and domains. The plan was to meet up in the park for a showdown. It was specified to be a fair, one against one, fight. The morning had arrived and I was rather nervous. Anything could happen. 'The Priests' and 'Oxton' gathered, whilst the two leaders shook hands. It was rather gruesome watching two people punching each other but Tony, someone we looked up to, had commenced the fighting with a member of the 'Oxton' gang. Every one joined in, kicking and punching until finally, bruised and bleeding, we went our separate ways. Thus, gang warfare became a way of life. I remember once being with Paul, also a member of the gang, and we found ourselves surrounded by youths outside the place where we both were training to be cooks. One of the group wanted to fight Paul. Fighting started; however, we managed to get away. On one occasion, some of us followed someone, and then attacked this person for causing trouble with one of our gang members. Often we used our bare hands, but weapons such as knives, chains and baseball bats were sometimes used. For example, when some of the gang members decided to walk through Oxton looking for other gangs to fight, to prove that we were the best and hardest of the gangs, many of the youths were carrying weapons. Then, seemingly out of nowhere, a car came screeching to a halt. Out of the car, poured several undercover police officers who started to chase us. I was soon caught and arrested. I remember being in the custody room and on the desks were many weapons, some of which were the evidence that demonstrated my guilt. I was charged under the Offensive Weapons Act. Interestingly, this made me pause and consider my actions and I started to become a bit more reluctant to fight with other people. Still, the gangs would continue to meet and fight. Sticks, bats and knuckle dusters were all part of our armoury. I remember going to Eastham to fight and we were out-numbered by lots of kids from a youth club who came running at us with snooker cues.

The fighting went on and so did my crimes. Not far from my house was a group of office buildings. I had decided to break in with a friend called Jeff. We went round the back and broke the window. Once in, I started to look around and eventually found a cash box. Unknown to us, a silent alarm had gone off which had signalled a response at the local police station. I remember looking out of the window and seeing a lot of police surrounding the building. Jeff and I had to find a way out. We both found the stairs and ran to the top of the building. At the very top was an attic in which I attempted to hide away. Jeff found his own hiding place. My heart was pounding and my sense of hearing was much heightened, as I strained to listen for any sounds that indicated someone was getting nearer. Suddenly, a light shone on my face and I was trapped. Ironically, the police officer was our next door neighbour. He was fair during the arrest and asked me, 'Why couldn't you have been doing something else like playing Snooker?' Sometimes there would be stories told of people breaking into large lorries. The news would spread and, before long, representatives from many local households would rush to the lorries to take part in looting, finding food or other things within the trailers.

Within 'The Priests,' Tony and Tom became like animals in a pack, each attempting to play the 'alpha male' role. I watched as Tom spent more time with his chosen friends and Tony with his. The split would come years later, but I started to see glimpses of the future of 'The Priests.' I had my fair share of fighting in the group, deciding the seniority and on one occasion, I picked up a stick and hit a guy called Terry. Terry was a little overweight and enjoyed his food and was more of Tony's friend, but a part of the 'Priests.' I cannot remember what the argument was over but he didn't talk to me until a few weeks later when it had blown over. Despite all of the bad things we were involved in, we adhered to a kind of honour code: the gang had a policy that we wouldn't break into occupied houses, neither would members take any drugs. This appealed to me and, for a long while, I went along with this.

The rest of the group, that didn't usually go out much, decided to go to an under-eighteens disco. I wanted to look my best and wore a bleached pair of jeans and a t-shirt. Paul and I kept together and did the usual thing, which was to try and impress the girls. There was a great song that night called 'The Boxer Beat,' which had a unique dance to go with it. After the disco we, as a group, started to dance along Conway Street only to be stopped by two special constables asking us to keep the noise down. Being the kind of person that I was, and not wanting to be told what to do (especially by the police, after what they did to my dad,) I continued to walk down the street. They called me but I still refused and then was grabbed and thrown against the billboard. I retaliated and kicked, punched and bit one of the officers. Before I knew it there were police cars everywhere and I was handcuffed and arrested, but still continuing to fight, until I was calmed down. I was charged with assault in 1983. I then had to wait for a court date at a juvenile court, which would be a trial. Statements were taken from those who were there on that night.

Whilst I was waiting for the trial, things carried on as usual. 'The Priests' continued at the youth club and at night we would light a small fire to keep warm on a field by Conway Street. It was part of our culture. It was around these small fires that we socialised and opened up to each other. It was also tradition to bring some potatoes with us and throw them on the fire wrapped up in tinfoil. At the end of the night, when the fires had burnt down, we would try and find the potatoes with a stick amongst the red ashes. I believed we weren't doing any harm, but the fire brigade would, on many occasions, arrive and put out the fires. This fueled anger in the youths and we attacked the fire engines with bricks and bottles, not thinking about the consequences of our actions.

We used to go to Grange Road Sports Centre to workout: not that easy for me as I was very skinny. It was quite a nostalgic thing being there, listening to eighties music in the café. , Every year Paul's parents would have a New Year's Eve party and we would all get drunk and sing the *Auld Lang Syne,* holding hands. Goodwill and all that, but it never lasted.

Whilst with 'The Priests,' occasionally, we would walk down Birkenhead precinct shops and if any young people stared at us because we were well known in the area, Paul and I would stop and hit them. This was to do with power and peer pressure; the need to prove oneself. It was a good feeling being in a gang; you felt invincible but it was not fun for those who came into contact with us on those days. Today I am certainly against such stupidity and what was a form of bullying. I would also shoplift and, after trying to take jewellery from T J Hughes, I got caught because, unknown to me, they had someone in the control room watching on CCTV. A store detective was then informed of the situation and told that I had placed jewellery in my pocket. As I walked out of the store, I was stopped. The store detective then escorted me into the store office where I had to wait until the police arrived. I was taken home and cautioned by the police.

I was very humorous when I used to steal. For instance, I broke into a school and decided to take a large piece of meat from the school kitchen. As I tried to get away I was caught by the police. Whilst in the car I heard a thump at the back of the car and as I turned around I saw the large piece of meat which the police had recovered from the bin. This incident went to trial and lasted all day. I was found guilty. My anger grew towards the police and any chance I got to abuse or shout abuse at them, I would. At

Birkenhead Market, a group of us were asked to move on, but I refused and was arrested by the police. I verbally abused the police and, on arriving at the police station, was pushed against the wall and punched by one of the officers, but thankfully the sergeant stopped him.

Birkenhead Park at night was a different atmosphere than the daytime. In the eighties the park had park police who would patrol the area. It was fun being chased by them most nights. We never got caught. The park, during the winter, was great fun. I remember once taking a coffin from the old mortuary at the back of our house (a bit morbid, I know!) and using it to slide down the snow-filled hills. As a teenager, I would take risks and one risk during the winter was to walk and skate on the park lake if it had frozen over. The amount of times I saw people go through the ice. Unfortunately, one winter, I foolishly took off my shoes and, with my socks on, started running on the frozen lake. Moments later, I noticed red spots on the ice. It was not long before I realised that it was blood... my blood. I had cut my foot open and, strangely, I didn't even feel whatever had caused the wound. I made my way to a phone box outside the park and phoned for an ambulance. It didn't take long for it to arrive and I was taken to Arrow Park Hospital where a nurse stitched my foot.

Finally, the trial regarding assault on the police had arrived and it was a long case. Witnesses were brought in and some of the statements contradicted what I had said. Now, up to this point I had been in and out of the police cells. The courts of justice had punished me in many ways. I had been fined, given suspended sentences, told to attend hours of community service and probation. My poor dad had spent many years having to come and bail me out, it was tiring for him. The juvenile court had no other option but to sentence me to 90 days in a detention centre... The short sharp shock.

CHAPTER 8

Short Sharp Shock

It was September 1982 and I was led away by the police officer, knowing that I would not see my family for many weeks. Aged fourteen and still at school, I was the first member of 'The Priests' to be sent to prison. The clanging of the keys, as the police officer unlocked the cell doors, brought home the harsh reality of prison life. There were other boys with me in the cell when I was locked in and we waited for a few hours before being transferred to Foston Hall - an old Victorian house that had been converted into a detention centre. My dad came to see me underneath the courts and I could not hold back the tears, breaking down in front of him. He was not new to prison, after spending eighteen years himself in and out of them. He advised me to keep my nose clean. After my dad left I was taken to a prison lorry outside with other youths and escorted to Foston Hall. I kept to myself but watched as two of the youths started fighting with each other. Like two savage dogs, they continued to argue and fight and I could feel my stomach churning as horrible thoughts about prison intruded into my mind. Finally, the lorry arrived and, as the doors opened, prison officers met us and we had to quick-march into Foston Hall. For the first two weeks prisoners were known as 'Inductions.' The regime was tough and difficult; this certainly included being away from home. On the first night a doctor had to do a medical check. I wanted to be sick and hopefully spend my days on the hospital wing but that was not to be and, instead, we were taken to our dormitory.

For the first two weeks we had the same routine, apart from weekends. We would wake up at around six-thirty, make our beds (known as our bed pack,) have a wash and then be led out into a courtyard to do an hour of drill or marching. Then, those under 16 (including myself,) went to school for half a day then worked; scrubbing floors until four o'clock. This was followed by the evening meal. At night we chose activities to do such as art, woodwork, social studies or sports, and then it was back for supper, which usually consisted of jam sandwiches and tea. The lights went out at nine o'clock and a red one was put on so that we could see if we needed the toilet. It was my first time in prison and, as I lay in bed, thoughts of home would dominate. I was missing my mum and dad. How was I going to get through Foston Hall? As I turned around and cuddled my pillow I could smell the aroma of freshness that came from the prison bed clothes. It wasn't long before I drifted of to sleep. This was a ritual for me during lights-out. I would reminisce about times spent with my family and visualise what life would be like once I got out. This took the focus off my being in prison for a few moments. In the morning we were woken up by one of the officers who came into the dormitory and picked up the bottom of the bed and let it drop. It was done in jest. On the way to getting your wash the aroma of bread being toasted would fill the Victorian corridors. Even now, as an adult, when I smell a cooked breakfast I am taken back to the mornings at Foston Hall.

Every day the deputy governor would come into our dormitory and do an inspection. If any dust or untidiness was found in the dormitory we were put on governor's report.

I received many letters, mostly from family. They had worked it so that there would always be someone writing to me. During the evenings (Monday to Saturday) letters would be given out after dinner. This was (and I know that I can speak for most - if not all - who were at Foston Hall) what we looked forward to the most. It was a time to escape the harsh reality of prison life and find out what friends and family had written. I was kept up to date about was going on with members of the family and friends. Sometimes, the young offenders would watch with envy as the officers called out my name more than once on any given night.

This meant I had a lot to read but it was always exciting. After two weeks we were assigned jobs for the rest of our time. Looking back, I can see how God was with me because I was given one of the best jobs called 'stores.' It was a highly paid job at £1.30 a week. My job duties included looking after the prisoner's clothes, toiletries and bedding. Each week I would collect the dirty washing and give out clean clothes. There was always some youth moaning at me if one of his shirts didn't have a button.

I felt proud and felt that this was definitely God intervening. I didn't know Him then but, looking back, you can see how He worked. I really got on with the prison officers and, at four o'clock on certain nights, was chosen to clean the staff offices. Bedtime was a time to reminisce and talk about the past and family to those who shared the dormitory. In the distance you could hear the traffic on the motorway, the only reminder at night of outside life. When you wanted to go to the toilet you had to get permission. On one occasion, an officer who was going off-duty came into the dormitory looking somewhat infuriated. Apparently, someone had been urinating out of one of the windows at the moment he walked past. He was not amused. I don't know if the culprit had been caught, but it certainly wasn't any of us in our dormitory. Just to clarify, each dormitory would have as many as eight, but no fewer than three young prisoners. At the end of a week, prisoners were given wages according to the amount of points they had been given on their score card. This was an incentive to keep us on track. Every morning and afternoon, not including the weekend, prison officers would score us, one to five, depending on our behaviour. This card would determine how much we were paid. I was, most of the time, paid a lot of money, about £1.30 - well it was a lot when you were in prison. I was fortunate that my friend, at that time, was known as the Daddy, a term given to a prisoner who ruled the prison. I was favorable with him because we had arrived at Foston Hall together.

One good thing that Foston Hall had was an army style regime which, apart from the marching, also had a gym and a very strict P.E. instructor. Every day, without fail, we had to go into the gym and workout. One thing that everyone hated was the wall-bars workout. You would all stand in the middle of the hall and, on the whistle, you had to climb to the top of the wall-bars in so many seconds. If you didn't do it then everyone would have to do it again. Circuit training was also incorporated. Circuit training involved many exercises to be done around the gym whilst someone else runs around the outside of two skittles. After he finished you could move onto the next exercise. I remember a fight in the gym with the instructor and a friend of mine, which was quite funny. I also found myself being kicked about by an officer in the courtyard all because I reminded him what was next on the timetable, making me out to be a 'smart alec.' The best officer was Mr. Pierson. He was great and everyone loved him. He was funny and really interested in everyone. I hated sport and, at the weekends, you would have a choice of football or rugby. The good news was that if you waited until all of the kits had gone you could go to the gym and have fun. So, most weekends, I waited until all of the kits were gone. There was, however, a tradition at Foston Hall. It was called 'the Run.' It was like the London marathon. The aim would be to run around Foston Hall eight times and you had to do it.

Privileges were also included as part of the prison system. Every so many weeks ties were given to the prisoners at Foston Hall who were well behaved and these came with certain privi-leges. For the first four weeks you had to wear a brown tie which indicated that you were new and were called 'inductions'. If, by chance, an officer took a liking to you, then you were given tasks that were generally given to prisoners with a red or green tie. Brown ties meant that your dormitory was inspected every day, you had to wait at the end of the dinner queue and you weren't given a pleasurable job. Instead, you had to scrub floors most days. If you were good after four weeks then a red tie would be given. This meant that you were trusted to a certain degree and you got a better job if you requested it. As well as going second in the dinner queue, you were allowed, after your meal, to go into the grade room, which was a separate dining area for those with the top ties which were green. In this room there was a table tennis game, snooker, board games and - not forgetting - the radio, which was something we looked forward to. Green ties were awarded after five weeks if you were excellent. Prisoners with a green tie could sit on the front row watching TV at the weekend or on a Thursday night Top of the Pops. As a green tie prisoner you were trusted to go around the prison without supervision. This felt good. Overall you were subjected to a regime that – yes, on the one hand - punished you, but, on the other, made you a better person - healthy and fit.

There were moments that became rather emotional, such as parents visiting every two weeks. I remember dad coming with mum and, as they walked through the door of the visitor's room, I broke down in tears. However, this was an opportunity to have tea with sugar. After all, you weren't allowed it at any other time, but I had a secret regarding sugar. Whilst at the stores warehouse (where as a red and green tie I worked,) I would have the task of making tea for the prison officers and some of them didn't mind me having a biscuit or sugar. It was not difficult to work out who my friends were because, during parade and inspection, one of the officers hinted at me and said, 'I notice a lot of new shoes have been given out.' As I was in charge of stores, the officer knew that I was showing favouritism and looking after my friends. He was very humorous about it.

If you were Church of England, you could go to church on a Sunday. In your locker you had your Sunday clothes. Although I, at the time, had not become Christian, I took the opportunity to use that privilege and went to church on Sunday mornings. It was much better than staying in the main prison. Prisoners were also given Gideon Bibles and, at the back, was a calendar. With some pencil lead, which I had to steal, I marked off the days in the calendar to help pass the time. The days before I was due to be released, I was allowed a hot bath. Up to that point, I had to use the showers. Walking through those gates the next morning was sad because I was so used to the regime and looked healthy and fit. What I didn't know was that I would be back a few years later.

CHAPTER 9

Behind the Scenes

Whilst I was at Foston Hall, 'The Priests' (the gang that I was in) had collected a lot of money to give to me and to take me for a celebratory drink. I arrived at Lime Street station in Liverpool and was greeted by Carl and Suzanne, my older brother and sister. It was great to see them. We hugged and started to talk about the family and they updated me with things that had been going on. They took me shopping and bought me new clothes. I was determined to go straight. It was good to be home with my mum and dad as I had missed them greatly, not to mention the good old home cooking. Walking into the house seemed strange because I had been away for some time, but it was not long before I adjusted to the house again. I was looking forward to meeting up with the gang - 'The Priests' - who, by now, had a group of girls that followed them. On the night of my release, Peter Brandrick (my play scheme youth worker) and the rest of 'The Priests' took me to a lovely restaurant called the "Blue Sky" in Birkenhead. I had steak and chips and then finished up at a pub which, coincidentally, was raided that night for underage drinking. I, thankfully, was not caught and made my way to Conway Street.

It was not long before I was back at school and Jean-Pierre was so pleased to see me. Not many people knew that I had been in prison. Jean-Pierre and I finished the last few months at school. After leaving school, we saw less of each other, but God had not finished with us yet.

After leaving school, I found a Youth Training Scheme job at the job centre, in catering, with my friend, Paul, from 'The Priests.' For many months we worked in the basement of the Sunderland and Highland Hotel in Eastham, learning how to be chefs. Paul and I were paid about £26.00 a week.

Although 'The Priests' had talked about their no drugs policies, I found myself sneaking off and befriending a drug dealer called Bill. Slowly I started to drift away from 'The Priests' because I wanted to explore this way of life. Bill used to deal marijuana and I was drawn into a world of drugs and stealing. It wasn't long before I was smoking cannabis and snorting speed. I slowly became a different person again and, although the dealer was caught and the flat boarded up, I started to look for other groups to take drugs with, with very little success. I drifted back into 'The Priests' and there were some new members that I knew from school. One of them I remembered from Conway Middle School called Ritchie. Without the others knowing, he introduced me to butane gas and instantly I became hooked. We would spend time with 'The Priests' and then sneak off to abuse solvents. I turned back to stealing again and was caught burgling a council building. It was a place where people would pay their rent money and I had decided to climb through the window and break in. It was late evening and I was rather nervous. As I was searching for cash, I heard the police outside and I lay on the floor pretending to be drugged. I can only assume that next door had heard me and had called the police. Anyway, I was caught by the police, as they shone their torches on me, and found myself in court again. Maybe it was for my own good. I called the solicitor and said to him, 'I know I am going away, but can you get the court to send me back to Foston Hall Detention Centre?' He kept his word and the court sentenced me to 90 days at Foston Hall. The second time wasn't bad at all. The first morning was interesting as I remember one of the prison officers (who I had built up a wonderful rapport with the last time I was at Foston Hall) saying to all of the other prisoners, 'This boy can be trusted.' This was because I had built up a good reputation with the prison officers last time and had been a model prisoner - despite one or two disastrous incidents, which I have already referred to. There were a few changes: they now had a video to show films, they didn't do drill any more and the officer who had kicked me had befriended me, even to the point of putting his arms around me during a visit from my mum and dad and telling them how good I was. The first thing to do, second time around, was to have a chat with Mr. Pearson and see if I could get my old job back at the stores. He did his best and I was back on stores again. My brother's friend, Matt, had also been sentenced at around the same time and we kept together. We would remain close after the Foston Hall experience.

One thing that makes the second time important was an incident that happened in the changing room. I was standing around and the new governor was being shown around the prison. He introduced himself to me and I noticed that his face was shining. I remember thinking to myself that I had never seen a face glow like that. It was many years later that I found out that this governor was a Christian.

On my release, my brother Carl picked me up in the car with Maxine his girlfriend (now his wife) outside the large secure gates of Foston Hall. He had stitches in his head and had been fighting with someone from our estate. One of the first things I did was to meet up with 'The Priests' and see my mum and dad at home. I had a girlfriend called Jane, who I had met just before I went in Foston Hall, and I went to visit her.

I noticed that 'The Priests' had started to disband and go their separate ways. There was still a friendly 'Hello' at the youth club when we met though. Stuart Melling was still at the youth club and we had a lot of catching up to do. I was looking forward to chatting to him. Matt, who was a friend of my brothers and a regular at Tranmere Rovers football matches, had also left Foston Hall and we both started to go to the 'Jimmies' (a nick name for a night club). We would drink a lot and take speed, which he would obtain from somewhere. We would both steal and, as usual, we were both arrested and charged with breaking and entering. It was through Matt that I met Peter Shaw: a very good looking boy with long hair and a generous nature. His mother lived not far from Conway Street. Peter worked at Birkenhead Market in a computer store. Instantly I knew he would become a good friend of mine, though this would later lead down a wrong path in my life.

When my mum and dad went out I would invite some of 'The Priests' to my house to drink and listen to music. The cannabis smoking had stopped, because I had found that drinking alcohol was exciting and something that you could get a hold of easier. It was not long before I noticed that the more I drank the more obnoxious I became, even to the point of throwing a brick at Jane, my girl friend at the time, and telling her that I didn't want her any more. I was pushing those that cared for me away and isolating myself. I was very immature and only lusted after girls. I wanted sex and, because of peer pressure, I needed a girlfriend to show off. I didn't care about their feelings at all as long as I got my sexual urges satisfied. I didn't think through the consequences on myself and on those that I was close to. I was sexually and emotionally immature and emotionally bonding with women was not something that I could even comprehend.

CHAPTER 10

The Downfall

I was sixteen years old and had got a job on a YTS training scheme at Rathbone Projects, on top of a Kebab shop in Liverpool near Lime Street Station, doing drama. It was a good course and taught me the basics about acting and I had my first taste of pantomime and played a dame, which was great fun. It was also embarrassing having to put tights on in front of the costume designers, who happened to be female. Previous students were Cathy Tyson and David Morrissey, who - to be honest - I hadn't heard of at the time. Peter, my new friend, used to gamble and this was the year that he inherited a lot of money after his grandma died and turned up at my workplace with money and cigarettes. I was also a gambler. I had started to gamble when I was about fourteen years old in the arcades and before I knew it I was addicted, I couldn't stop. My wages from the YTS would all go on gambling. My mum had a bad time with me. I didn't pay rent. However, she didn't tell my dad and protected me. I found out that Peter enjoyed solvents and, thus, my downfall began, as I got back involved with that old habit. For the next year, every week we would meet up at old garages sniffing gas. It started off with one bottle, then two and went on to a whole box of butane gas. My personality was changing; I was becoming anaemic and started looking pale all the time. I had no pride in myself. Sometimes I would wear the same clothes for days. We would go back to Peter's house and steal brasses off the walls and sell them at an auction. Gambling had taken over our lives. I enjoyed the flashing lights and the possibility of winning more money. I did not see the consequences that lay ahead for me if I continued down this path. I didn't even think that far ahead.

We went from gas to paint (although the paint didn't work).

An old friend called Lee started to notice the change in my behaviour. For example, my temper was much worse, resulting in him getting fed up with me and telling me that he was going home. I was also possessive of Lee and became bitter and angry towards him. I picked up some glass and sliced my arm to emotionally blackmail him, so that he would not go home. However, he was not amused and left, leaving me to make a decision regarding going to hospital. The hospital asked questions about the slashes on my arm, but I said that I was attacked as I was too ashamed to tell the truth. Even now, when I catch a glimpse of the faded scars, I realise how silly I was and what alcohol can do to a person if they abuse it.

Around this time, I became involved in the occult and found that I became attracted to graveyards at night and enjoyed the eeriness of the gravestones. It was the power that one got from taking friends to cemeteries and frightening them. Whilst at home I would try to contact the dead with a few friends, but no one ever talked to us. I was a creative person and found that having people watch and become frightened was great fun at the time. I enjoyed the attention, but it was all an act. However, messing around with the occult is dangerous and should not be taken too lightly. I was foolish and now realise that the occult is something that you should not get involved with. I used to paint pictures of grave-yards and, at one time, someone had stolen a coffin from a mortuary at the back of our house on Conway Street. As a joke, I climbed inside and asked my friends to put the lid on me. I then jumped out as people gathered around the coffin in the estates playground (which had swings and a round-a-bout). I was becoming weird and strange, in my opinion, but, looking back, I can categorically say that most of what I did was for attention. As someone who enjoyed performing and watching horror movies I would mimic the voice of the child in the horror film, *The Exorcist*, and - again - it was to impress people.

People and friends ostracised me, others kept their distance. I was not getting on with my parents. In fact, my dad painted 'Drugs Kill' in red paint on my wall in the hope that it would stop me from taking drugs. Stuart Melling would occasionally call in to see me at home and my parents would ask him if I would be all right and grow out of this lifestyle. Stuart felt in his heart that I would and it would be a matter of time before this lifestyle would stop and a new direction and interests would take over. Stuart felt confident in saying this.

I started getting really bad headaches. My heart would pound all the time. One night, after going to the night club, I decided to break into a shop and see if there was any money. I had been drinking and did not like not having money in my pockets. I looked around and it was not long before I found a cash box. As I climbed out of the window to make my way down the street, an off-duty police officer (on the other side of the road) came after me and was successful in making an arrest. Whilst at the police cells, a decision was made to keep me in overnight and for me to appear before a Saturday court. After breakfast I was led down some long corridors and up stairs and stood before the court as the charges of theft was read out. It was agreed that I would be remanded until Tuesday of that week. I was sent to Risley Remand Centre for three days. It was a not a nice place, but in the cell I cried out to God to help me. A few days later I was back in the court room. The court decided to give me bail and I was released. My friends from 'The Priests' (including my good friend Paul) were there to support me. After realising how depressing and horrible an adult prison was, I was determined to go straight. How was I going to do this? My body was suffering from the results of drugs, such as pale skin, headaches, loss of weight and the stigma of occasionally being seen as a drug addict. My brother was good to me and on many occasions would give me pep talks about the reality of taking drugs. He would also help by giving me his old clothes, which looked great on me, as I was not in a position to buy any new clothes. I would also go to the pub with

him to have a quiet drink, not too much. I needed help and God
was about to reveal part of his plan

CHAPTER 11

A New Beginning

Although 'The Priests' didn't meet as a gang, they had matured and would gather to chat with youths in St. Werburgh's Square in Birkenhead. One day, whilst out of prison, to my surprise Jean-Pierre (my old school friend) visited me whilst I was with my friends, chatting in a group in town. He asked if we could talk so we went into the St. Werburgh's Church graveyard (opposite Beatties) and sat under the cross of Christ. Jean-Pierre did not hide the fact that he was a Christian and was very open about Christ coming back. His parents were Jehovah's Witnesses, but Jean-Pierre had become a Christian and, as he talked, I realised that I too needed help. I said that if God could help me become an actor then I would accept him into my life. I said a prayer and didn't have any dramatic feeling or change. I was an immature Christian and, at first, was thinking about what God could do for me. However, God - in his grace - saw my heart and was patient. The next week, without fail, Jean-Pierre arrived at my house to take me to church. I remember walking up Willmar Road in my dad's suit and entering an old church that looked derelict from the outside. The brickwork was old and the windows looked like they hadn't had any work done on them for some time. However, to my surprise, we entered through a side door in a building that had - to my knowledge - been built many years later after the main church. I was greeted by a gentleman who seemed friendly and he shook my hand. The hall had a smell of wood and, rather than pews, it had chairs. It was a charismatic church; lively, with people speaking in strange languages. We were made to feel very welcome. The Pastor, at that time, was Robert Smith. He had lived in South Africa and had a wife and three children. The hall was small in size and so was the congregation. For the next few weeks, I started to become very outgoing with my new found faith and was very zealous. If I could attend meetings, I would and I looked forward to regularly attending Willmar Road. On the Sundays that I could attend, I would dress smartly, wearing my dad's suits because I hadn't purchased my own due to financial difficulties.

Ian and Joan Ogilvy were also part of the congregation and Ian, himself, had come from a background similar to myself. I enjoyed Ian's company as we had similar backgrounds. It wasn't long before I felt that there was a need for me to be surrounded by more young people of my own age. The problem with Willmar Road, during the eighties, was that there weren't any young people attending apart from Jean-Pierre and the pastor's three daughters. I had heard of the Wirral Christian Centre (a large charismatic church, which had a large congregation) and I wanted to be with people my own age who also loved God, so I made a decision with Jean-Pierre to attend.

Back at home, my parents were noticing a change, but it was to the other extreme. I was locking myself, with the Bible, in the bedroom. Jean-Pierre and I were zealots. I was over the top and - looking back - I can see that I was a hypocrite. On the one hand, I went to church and then, after the service, I went to an off-license to buy alcohol. I still needed to free myself from the old habits that God was showing me were not acceptable anymore. I thought that attending a church was a good start, but still there was more I needed to change.

Slowly, I started to take notice of my appearance (even though I still had a skinhead and looked aggressive). My anger was still there but I managed to control it on certain occasions. I found sleeping difficult: I was frightened to go to sleep because I may never wake up; I had a terrible fear of dying. For the next few weeks I tried various ways of getting off to sleep. I would write poetry and notes about God through the night and eventually drift off to sleep. I was having withdrawal symptoms from drugs and occasionally found myself tempted. Lying in bed on many occasions I would ask God to take me, that very night, to heaven. I thought that maybe God wanted to take my life - how wrong I was. I would physically be shaking at night, but found a ritual that lasted some time. In this ritual I would hold onto a large cross in my bed and pray for God to help. The drugs had damaged me and time would be the healer. However, these sensations started to improve as the weeks went on. There was a time when Jean-Pierre's mother mentioned my skin being pale whilst at Jean-Pierre's home. She suggested that I take some tanning cream, which had come from one of the woman magazines. I took up the offer and that night, in the bathroom, put it on. The next morning when I awoke, I became very excited at the thought that my face was lovely and brown. However, when I looked in the mirror, I was shocked to see that, rather than looking brown, I was orange. It took time to fade, but I decided to sit in the sun for hours to get a tan in the hope of never becoming pale again. I kept this up for a long time.

The drinking still continued, so did the over-the-top evangelism. I would spray red paint on arcades and sex shops and put Christian tracts in most phone boxes. I was an aggressive fundamentalist, stepping out of the boundaries of God's will in an extreme way.

The Christian Centre was very large and led by Paul Epton, a man of God but also - in my opinion – a man who looked like a model from a catalogue, dressed in his fine suits. He was powerful at preaching and very humorous. I also met Vincent and Donna, who became very close to me as the years went on and very supportive during my single years. Vincent had come from a background of the occult and, at this time, was very sensitive as a new Christian. Donna (although part of the group of Christian youths) had not begun a relationship with Vincent. This would happen, with the help of a friend, later on. I started to genuinely enjoy my Christianity. I was still going to nightclubs, smoking and drinking, but my heart was genuine. For the next few years God started the process of healing me. I started to attend the youth club again, this time as a Christian. It took a lot of courage to do this. My hair had grown and was now in the style of a young Cliff Richard. Stuart Melling was rather surprised when I told him that I was a Christian. He attended church himself and had some understanding of faith.

Our youth pastor at the centre was Mike Haynes. He was tall, good looking and a gentleman. He loved young people and he had built up a rapport with schools in the area. The youths would sometimes travel to Wales and have a lovely time of fellowship and worship - something I miss today. I would also use these times to look for a relationship, hoping to meet a special Christian lady. The only problem was, I was too over the top and assumed that, if I could get their attention, they would like me, which didn't go to plan. I was trying too hard. I suppose I didn't know how to be myself, as I had changed beyond recognition.

CHAPTER 12

Acorn of Acting

Within me was a desire to learn more about life. I felt that there was so much I had yet to experience. God had been working and I felt the need to go back to education, realising how important education is. The acorn of acting started to grow and also my love for the theatre. I enrolled at Withens Lane College and did the performing arts course, which was very exciting. I was young and thought that I knew what acting was all about, but I was wrong and knew that I had a lot to learn. The college had provided a bus to collect people. One morning, whilst sitting by myself, a gentleman sat next to me. He was slim and looked like an actor. He introduced himself as Ron Gittins. God had intervened and this man was about to play an important part in my life, not only as a person but as a Christian. During our conversation it emerged that he had been a member of the Elim Church and he had known Paul Epton many years before I attended. Ron had come from a Methodist background. He was very well-spoken. I remember wishing that I could speak like him. He was also on the performing arts course and in his first year. Over the next few years our friendship grew. Having been limited, as a child, of a quality education, communicating, writing, knowledge of culture or fine arts was alien to me. Ron, with my permission, started to tutor me. It reminded me of Richard Burton and his teacher: they would go off to the hills and recite poetry and read. I was excited and most nights looked forward to Ron crossing the open field in front of our house. This was where the row of houses and the mortuary, that I referred to earlier in the book, stood, but had now been demolished. Our houses were turned around after a council makeover to improve the area: the backs were now the fronts. In fact, many changes had happened, not just to our estate, but also to the new houses that had been built. Grange Road was looking more modern. The old market had burnt down and a new one had been built in its place. We now had pound coins, CDs and mobile phones. Life was not the same in the nineties.

Whilst at Withins Lane College I noticed that Ron's manner had changed and that he had started to withdraw, resulting in him finding it difficult to focus on his lines from *A Midsummer Night's Dream*. He had confided in me, conveying his interest for a female student in the same year. Ron, at the time, wanted to show that he was a gentleman, however this caused problems with the student in question: she had refused to have the door opened by him and he had become withdrawn and despondent. Ron had conveyed his struggle with *A Midsummer Night's Dream* and I realised that he was asking for help, even if it was not in an overt way. Together we spent time rehearsing his part as 'Egeus' until he felt confident. Ron showed a personal interest in me to educate and widen my mind in arts, Greek, and literature (something that I was eager to know about). Ron would arrive at my home around eleven o'clock at night. Sometimes, he would have a classical video with him which we watched into the early hours. Ron enjoyed the Roman classics such as *Ben-Hur, The Fall of the Roman Empire, Spartacus* and many more. I was learning so much about communication, culture and even carrying around a piece of paper with new words on. I had a northern accent and wanted so much to speak like Ron, whom - I believed - was more refined. My vowels were flat and, over time, Ron helped me to develop southern ways of speaking, where some vowels are long. I would, on many occasions, question the way certain words were pronounced and, with Ron's help, learned how to pronounce the words that I thought were important to my development. Going to the park and reading out loud, with people walking past, was frightening, but fun and helped with projection of the voice. This was a very important aspect of being an actor. Ron had started to introduce me to different people from all walks of life to build my self confidence. At one time, I was left standing in a courtroom with a solicitor next to me to see if I could successfully hold my own and communicate with her. This was a test for me. She didn't know my past and I had changed my voice a little so I didn't sound flat. We started to converse, after Ron had introduced us, but all was not going too well. I felt embarrassed, intimidated and I knew that I had a long way to go if I wanted to be a gentleman. I wanted to have the self confidence to talk to people from different walks of life without feeling inferior and unrefined.

CHAPTER 13

Dark Night of the Soul

I did make friends at the Christian Centre: one person I met called Mark seemed very spiritual. We became friends and it was nice to meet someone like-minded... Or so I thought. I was completely free from drugs - praise God - and Mark (who was unaware that I had been involved in taking cannabis and other drugs) invited me to his house, after seeing me depressed, to cheer me up. He gave me some cannabis to my surprise and somehow I knew that it was not the right feeling. After all, it was a Christian offering it this time. However, I was low and decided to have some. I had a bad reaction because I had taken too much and found myself in hospital. The next few weeks after this period were difficult with many panic attacks and anxieties. I reported him to the Christian Centre and he eventually left. God turned it around: I found that I didn't want to drink alcohol anymore either and I became teetotal as well. I cried out to God and help came in the way of drama back at Withens Lane doing another performing arts course. I had stopped smoking and, whilst at Withens Lane College, I met Mr. T, who I will call Mark. At first, he seemed genuine but as the months went on I found him even more demanding and, sadly, wanting my attention. Sometimes he would stop and cry if I wanted to be with other friends and could not understand if I spent time elsewhere. He would wait for me outside my parent's house. Once he even attacked me with a screwdriver because I was not at his beck and call; I was emotionally drained. This friendship wasn't Christian and wasn't healthy. We were doing Pygmalion and I had to drop out because of my ingrown toenail. Mark told me that he had been a male nurse, but I found that difficult to believe and I was right. Anyway, one night in the house he said he would have to look at the toe and pulled out a stanley knife, which frightened me. That was the last I had to do with him, he was a pathological liar and I kept my distance from then on. At that point, I started to realise that friendships can be fraught with danger and difficulties.

Ron Gittins continued to help me and, after doing a BTEC in acting, I became serious about professional training. It was time to audition at a professional drama school. Stuart Melling from 'The Dolly' had helped to set up an organisation called 'WAY' (Wirral Association for Youth). Whilst I was looking around and deciding on drama schools, I joined WAY. It was exciting and I was, once again, working alongside Stuart Melling. I enjoyed his company. Slowly my desire to act became insignificant and I wanted to become a youth worker myself. It was a time when Wirral was allocated funds for youth and 'WAY' had a voice in how these funds would be spent. It was a fun time; certainly being elected young person's representative was an honour. I had privileges and would sit with different movement bodies and parties at the town hall. Visiting youth groups and talking to young people was also part of the job. I was starting to understand government policies and the terminology that people in government were using and was able to speak in front of important people. God had transformed me from someone who was oppositional to authority, to someone who was trying to make young people's lives better through authority.

It was an exciting time with 'WAY' and we had many adventures in the white minibus. In 1991 Granada TV had a 48 hour fundraising event, which myself and other members of youth groups participated in. We had to push a tyre around Wirral Country Park. A lot of money was raised over those two days. One night, sitting in Stuart Melling's car, came a defining moment for me: he looked at me in the face and said very loudly 'You are an actor not a youth worker,' realising that, although it was good to work with young people, I should not be neglecting my talents. He was right. I had been deviating off the path and needed to get back on. I realised that I had to get serious about my future.

RADA, the Royal Academy of Dramatic Art, was a famous drama school and trained the best, so I decided to audition, taking Ron with me for support. My voice was being developed and I had two audition pieces, which I had learnt during the BTEC Course at Cheshire School of Dance and Drama. We travelled on the National Express and arrived in London on time. I had been to London once before with a friend from the Birkenhead Institute School called Richard back in the eighties. This was the moment that my life could change. There I was, walking through those famous doors on Gower Street. Once in, I was asked to sit and wait to be called. Before I knew it I found myself in front of a distinguished gentleman with a student with him. I performed a piece from *Hamlet* (the Claudius, 'Oh, my offence is rank' speech) and a Chekhov piece. It was a joy to be told that he enjoyed the piece and that I should get a job to earn money, but not give up auditioning. I was not offered a place at that time and was upset but managed to pick myself up and continue to audition. Every few months I would buy a National Express ticket and head to London to audition at other schools including, CENTRAL, LAMDA, and ALRA. Two of these said, 'No' and Alra decided to recall me, but unfortunately I was not successful the second time. Distressing as it was, I was encouraged by Ron not to give up. Our tuition continued and my voice started to change. At times I sounded like Richard Burton and other times a various selection of others. My brother, at the time, was not amused and, leaning over to my mum one day at the Christmas table, said, 'What is up with his voice?' I was not perfect and I even felt embarrassed at times as my voice was developing as an actor, but I wanted to have the right tools. My voice was important to get right.

Vincent and Donna had now married, which was great, and I had come across a Christian Drama School in London called the School of Creative Ministries. What did I have to lose? I filled in the application form and sent it off. Whilst I was waiting, I had joined the choir at the Christian centre and enjoyed being out front singing until, for whatever reason, I was told to stand down. I think it was to do with the way that I dressed. Mind you, I did wear jeans and t-shirts whilst in the choir. I was upset and spent the night sulking at Vincent and Donna's who were very supportive. They even had me over on New Year's Eve because I was alone without a girlfriend. Donna had a quest, which was to find me a woman - a Christian of course. Although this was not an easy task, she took on the challenge.

Jean-Pierre had started photography and he was very good at it. He used to have his dark room in his bathroom and took many photographs as I progressed as an actor. He wanted to chart my journey. It was time to travel to London for the audition at the School of Creative Ministries (SCM). This was based at Kensington Temple; a very large church in London. It was Monday 12th July 1993 and my audition was on the 13th July, which meant that I travelled on the night bus. I didn't sleep well and was very tired. It took many hours before the bus finally arrived at London Victoria coach station. I could not wait to get off the bus and stretch my legs and made my way to the toilets at the station to refresh myself with a good wash. My next task was to travel to Notting Hill Gate on the tube, then to make my way to a large building known as Kensington Temple. I was greeted by a receptionist who directed us to the audition room. It was rather a large space and at one end of the room were David Grant and Carrie Grant. I had no idea who they were. To me, they were just two Christian teachers making judgments about whether we were good enough, or had the potential, to learn our craft. It was a workshop audition and involved dancing, singing and acting. Throughout the day, alongside other potential artists, I was put through my paces. I didn't mind dancing or singing but my discipline at that time was acting and this was the moment that I had been waiting for. Here was an opportunity to show David and

Carrie that I had what it takes to be a student at their performing arts school. My heart started to pound as I made my way to the performance space and recited 'Oh my offence is rank' from *Hamlet*. It was not perfect but I had done all that I could using every technique that I had learned. I knew that I had a long way to go as an actor. I remember reading many accounts of actors who had found it difficult auditioning at various drama schools including RADA: one of which was Kenneth Branagh. For now, all that mattered was being accepted into the SCM. Carrie and David's response to my audition pieces were positive. Carrie told me that I was nearly ready and that the school would help. It turned out that the school would help in many ways; offering a grounding in Christian truths (which was so important as a Christian artist in a secular world) and professional training in all aspects of the performing arts. Like so many actors, my mind was in overdrive and was being monopolised by thoughts of 'would they accept me?' or 'What if I was terrible?' During the interview David told me that he felt that I had been rejected in the past. He was right. I broke down crying, suffering from so much rejection and feeling low in confidence. After the interview I had one final meeting with someone called Jumoke Fasola, who talked about the finances and costs of the terms at SCM. It was not long before I was due back on the National Express to travel back to Birkenhead. It was now a waiting game and, for many days, I would be plagued with negative thoughts about being rejected. Then one morning in July 1993, a letter arrived and it was addressed to me. As I opened it I could see the letterhead, which indicated to me that it was from SCM. I slowly started to read the first line, as sometimes you can tell whether or not you had been accepted just by the way they start the letter. Suddenly, my eyes were drawn to the line that said it all: 'We are delighted to confirm that you have been accepted into the School of Creative Ministries.' At last I was accepted into a drama school, this was exactly what I believed God wanted me to do. Exciting months lay ahead as I tried to raise the money to pay for the fees. This was going to be a new adventure. SCM would start in the October of 1993 and continue until the summer of 1994. I found out that Carrie had been a presenter on TV and David Grant was a member of a band called *Lynx*. I was not successful at raising the money and, three days before I was due to attend the School of Creative Ministries, I screamed at God, 'What a horrible father you are. You get me into drama school but have not provided.' I should not have said that, but at that moment the phone suddenly rang and it was Chico, a lady from School of Creative Ministries. She told me that she was fasting for students. That night, I had a vision of a vicar and youth worker handing me a cheque. As I entered the doors to Charing Cross Youth Club that night (now run by someone called Tim. Stuart Melling had moved on to work somewhere else), I was called into the office and the Methodist vicar and Tim handed me a cheque for a few hundred pounds. This was a miracle and many more would soon happen. My Christian faith soon became exciting. I was thankful to God. The moment arrived and, with my bags packed for London, I said goodbye to dad, mum and family. I was going to be away for some time, apart from the end of term times. I had a little more experience as an actor. My voice had changed, in fact, my flat vowels were now sounding like southern vowels. I looked out of the window of the National Express coach and my stomach started to churn. I was frightened and in my hand I had a diary. On the first page I wrote, 'the journey has begun.'

CHAPTER 14

The Journey

After about an hour on the bus I felt much calmer. It was a Sunday 3rd October 1993 and SCM was beginning the following day. It was late afternoon when I arrived in London and I made my way to Kensington Temple Church in Kensington. I didn't have any accommodation and, with about thirteen pounds left after paying the first term's course fees, I had no idea what lay ahead. I was greeted by Chino and mentioned that I needed to find accommodation. She seemed rather upset that I hadn't found anywhere. Not far from the church were a few hotels, so I managed to find one with breakfast only. The room was at the top of the stairs and only had a bed and table in it. It was not a great place but at least it was somewhere to stay for the night. Sleep was good and the next morning I made my way to drama school. As I walked the street looking for the building, I thanked God that Peter Hutchison met me. He had trained at the London Academy of Dramatic Art and was our acting teacher. Together we went in. First day nerves kick in as we were all introduced to the course contents and the teachers. The first day was an intro-duction and the day I met Chris, who became a good friend. He was a great singer and piano player. Ian Sparks was also to become a good friend; the ladies were great as well.

The structure was simple: nine-thirty to one o'clock, five days a week at drama school then a walk to church to the bible school, which was part of the course. David and Carrie started to ingrain in us that working in entertainment as a Christian was not a problem: we were called to be salt of the earth and our talents could be used in the secular world. Over the past few years, many Christians (not all) didn't take too kindly to a Christian working in television, certainly secular. At SCM it was encouraged. At the end of the first day, I needed accommodation and God intervened with Gary. Gary was Indian and worked late nights in a bakery. He invited me to his home where I stayed for two weeks sleeping on the floor. The house where Gary lived had many other people living there and I sometimes had to get up at around five thirty in the morning just to get a shave and wash. If I didn't, I would have had to wait a long time, as the other people were using the bathroom. It was difficult, but what else could I do? One night, during the two weeks, I decided to look for other accommodation in London. I had been given an address of possible accommodation near Notting Hill Gate, so I set out and caught the tube to this place. However, it was not what I was looking for. It was similar to a YMCA and had dormitory style living. My heart sunk as I made my way back to Gary's house.

SCM was hard work and discipline was important. If you arrived late to start class you could not start the class unless you had good reason. Carrie and David trained us over the next few months and we were growing. Yvonne Morley (now a voice teacher at a major drama school) took us through our paces and one person we always looked forward to seeing was Nigel Goodwin. He had trained at the very school that I had wanted to go to: RADA. He was a friend of Sir Cliff Richard and was instrumental in setting up the 'Art Centre Group' with David Winter in the sixties. This was a group of Christians who came together to talk and debate about the arts. The ACG today has hundreds of members and are doing great work. It also spawned other groups such as "Genesis Arts", and 'Christians in Entertainment.' 'Christians in Entertainment' was set up by Chris Gidney, an entertainer and someone who worked behind the scenes. He was gentle and would be encouraging. He travelled around the country, visiting artists and running Bible studies. He has written many books about well-known celebrities and their stories regarding Christianity. Sally Goring was part of the pastoral team. She was a great prayer warrior and very encouraging. I remember Chris phoning me up and telling me to make sure that this journey into the acting profession was what I really wanted. I think he knew then I was determined from that moment on. 'Christians in Entertainment' was to play a huge part in my life. Nigel Goodwin had a great voice and we would listen to him for hours, talking about arts and the Bible. Little did I know that many years later I would have further meetings with him.

David and Carrie had been asked to participate in a gospel evening at the London Palladium and needed to choose a few of us to sing. I remember the moment in St. Peter's Hall that they chose their singers. I listened and gave up hope. After all, my chosen subject was Drama. God had other plans. Chris, with a loud voice, said, 'Christopher can sing.' Carrie and David called me over and then began weeks of training. We had to perform two songs with David (who was documented by BBC 1 in a programme called 'Simply the Best;' a short documentary about he and Carrie). At this time I had to leave Gary's and, in a way, I was pleased to get off that floor. God once again intervened and I found myself a house with the help of a dear friend, Beverly (a lovely actress at SCM). She had a friend called Patsy who had two houses and I was blessed with her second one. It had a garden, three bedrooms, a large kitchen and living room. One bedroom was, on rare occasions, given over to family but most of the time I had the house to myself. I was short of money and, therefore, prayed and somehow money came into my hand through the students at SCM.

The London Palladium Show had arrived and, on the night, the house was packed. I remember rehearsing and singing in the corridor next to the dressing room and met the late Roy Castle who had had cancer and was recovering. He was top of the bill. Wendy Craig was also doing a sketch. It was a fantastic night, with a standing ovation at the end. We also performed at the London Dock Arena with David and Carrie. So at last I found some recognition on TV and the theatre. I still had a long way to go. Inside of me I was deeply lonely and in need of finding some companionship in a girl. Yes, I wanted female company. Ron had come to visit me at drama school and said, months later, that I looked very drained. It was difficult and many times I cried and wanted to give up. David and Carrie encouraged me and, one day, David and I went for a walk. He is such a nice person and I admired him, not only for making a stand for his faith but also for being real and working in the secular media. He put his arm around me, advised me not to give up, as I was a fine actor.

Those words of comfort were, and still are, something that I would think about when I felt down. It was 1994 and I was sitting at my lodgings in Catford one night when I received a phone call from Vincent to tell me that Richard, a dear Christian friend, had died. I could not believe it. Richard and I met at the Christian Centre Church and he was very popular with the girls. I made sure that I spent time with him because of the women, but I genuinely liked him as a friend. I remember going to SCM and exploded in anger at one of the teachers because she said that I was screwed up. This was because I was grieving over my friend and I was also dealing with the issue that I wanted to go to a secular drama school instead of SCM. She was upset and said, 'look, you are getting professional training here, if you want to go on why haven't you been turning up for my lesson?' I told her that my friend had died and she told me that I was screwed up. I assumed that she meant something like twisted or something stronger.

I didn't want to go on any more and, whilst we were rehearsing for the Easter show, I broke down on the stage and walked out, never to return to SCM as a student. My friends were shocked and Carrie and David were too. I would, in years to come, see them again. God had a lot of work to do in my life. Patsy had told me that she needed the house where I was living and I didn't know what to do. I remember one night, lying in bed in the lodgings, and waking suddenly. I asked God, 'Will I go To RADA?' Inside of me very clearly I heard, 'Yes.' It was my thought. I was now positive. 'Yes, I will go to RADA.' Anyway, my problem was that I had nowhere to go; I didn't want to go home. I was on a mission to becoming an actor.

Chris, my friend from SCM, had introduced me to Richard Ford, who lived in a picturesque village in Warlingham. He was tall and reminded me of Mathew Kelly, although he didn't think so. He had been an actor and enjoyed the theatre and arts. I had stayed over once, a few months before, and been to his house once or twice with guests, so I phoned him in the hope that he could help me out with accommodation. To my relief, he agreed and I packed my bags only to return to Patsy's once more for something that was a miracle blessing.

CHAPTER 15

Living in the Country

Croydon is a large place and looks like a city. Some say that it is a city, just without a cathedral. I was picked up by Richard in his car and taken for something to eat. Richard's house was next to a large open field and only a bus ride away from Croydon, my main shopping place for the next year. I had my own room and was excited about being there. Richard was great fun, being an actor himself, but also enjoyed quiet moments of solitude, which was difficult when I was around.

I used to worry a lot about being underweight but the problem disappeared as Richard was a good cook and his portions could fill a family. One of the things that I remember was Richard's improvisations (or spontaneous outbursts). I was in the living room once and he had put on this strange voice. In one hand he held a large axe. This was like a scene from *The Shining*, but I knew that he was play-acting and, before I knew it, he had chased me around the house. We would have lots of laughs together. He was a big child at heart and I used to enjoy Thursdays. It was shopping day and we would travel into Caterham to shop at Waitrose. This was also where Richard, at times, went to church and where I met some of his friends. One was a singing teacher and encouraged me, one day, as I tried to sing 'Bring Him Home' from *Les Miserables*. After shopping we would go home and enjoy a hot chocolate in front of the fire watching a video. Richard and I grew spiritually together as prayer and bible reading became a part of life. He was protective of me but knew that I had to mature in one or two areas. I had slipped back into wanting attention again and it was, at times, wearing him out. I made an effort by allowing him time alone.

This gave me the opportunity to travel around Croydon and

look for someone special in my life. Saturdays were courting days for me. I would make sure that I looked well-groomed, as now, one thing that had changed was a new interest and pride in myself. Appearance was important. I just needed to work on hair styles. If I couldn't afford gel I would use face cream, but I never got it right and my hair, at times, looked like a slanted rooftop. It was exciting being around Croydon; walking up and down in the hope of getting noticed, but returning home to Richard's would burst the bubble of finding a woman. This was nothing to do with Richard, it was about arriving home unsuccessfully. Richard also shared my joy of travelling and enjoyed finding a place to pray, such as on a hillside.

We both attended a church in Croydon most Sunday evenings, which was very charismatic and also the church of Chris from SCM. It was good to see Chris again and our friendship blossomed. The youths, at times after the church, would travel to McDonalds and one time to Brighton. These were educational and a time to develop relationships. The acorn of acting was calling me again and I auditioned for a major drama school called ALRA. This time I got through to the second round and had to travel back weeks later to audition. This was a step in the right direction, but unfortunately I did not get in.

My time with Richard had come to an end and it was time to move on, but not without an interesting funny experience. Richard and I had decided to go for a meal and I was very fussy (and still am). He had taken a wrong turn on a road that was being resurfaced. In front of me I could see a steam roller coming towards us, but Richard kept driving. Workmen suddenly came at us and screamed, 'Stop the car! Stop the Car!' My immediate reaction was to forget Richard and get out of the car. It was hilarious, but also frightening. God had his hand on us and we managed to get past them all right. I was frightened and it reminded me of the car accident that my parents and I had had a few months earlier: Carl, my brother, had invited me to be

Godfather to Natalie, his daughter, and, after leaving the function room, my dad (who was driving) was hit by another car. I felt like I was in a bubble. Suddenly I had the strength to get out of the car and stop the cars, run back and get help from my brother. Mum and dad were shook up a little but not serious. Thank God for his intervention.

It was not long before I was looking for another drama school. Whilst in Birkenhead with my parents I came across the Lee Strasburg Studio, which was in London and being advertised in the Stage newspaper. Lee Strasburg was known as a method teacher. Dustin Hoffman, Robert De Niro, Al Pacino were said to have trained under him. The method school had been set up in London and I applied, got some funding and was accepted. As usual, I had no accommodation. I phoned Sally Goring from 'Christians in Entertainment' and mentioned that I would be training at the Lee Strasburg Studio and needed accommodation. Prayer is powerful: I was a young Christian and my faith was exciting. Not long after the phone call, Sally phoned back to say that she knew of an actor who was going on tour with the National Theatre and was looking for someone to look after the house. His cottage was at the back of an old Victorian house in Streatham, near Brixton. We arranged to meet up and I agreed to live there during his tour, this was perfect for me as I could now train at Lee Strasburg.

I was taught a lot about method acting which included 'Emotion Recall:' using whatever you had as a person to help with creating characters. Our teacher was Marilyn Hill, who had been in *The Godfather* movies with Lee Strasburg. I remember doing one exercise where she asked me to be a child and bring back emotions from my childhood. I started swearing and getting angry with her. It was role-play and worked; I tapped into realism. Some exercises went a bit too far in my opinion. I found it draining, tapping into the past, when I knew that God wanted me to look forwards not backwards.

Due to a fall-out over leaving the heating on at the actor's house, I left the cottage early and went back to Richard for about four weeks. Whilst shaving, after leaving the actor's house, I said to God, 'If you want me to leave Lee Strasburg, then I pray Sally from 'Christians in Entertainment' will phone right now.' Suddenly, the phone rang and it was Sally. I never went back. It wasn't the right school for me. However, I took some of the training techniques with me. After four weeks, I went back home to Birkenhead and I got a private drama tutor. I was determined to get into the right drama school. The School of Creative Ministries was a good school but it wasn't right for me. God, however, had allowed me that experience which I needed.

One thing I need to mention is how, through prayer one day at Richard's, I cried out to God for a financial miracle and, soon after, the phone rang and it was my old landlady telling me that there was a cheque for over £800 at my old lodgings. I did not hesitate. I got a bus to her house and it was true. 'Thank you, God,' I said.

CHAPTER 16

Open Doors

Ernest Hopner was a great drama teacher and used to have a school at Blue Coat Chambers in Liverpool. He had trained at LAMDA and had an actor's voice. You knew immediately that he was an actor when you met him because of his look and presence. I learnt a lot from him and polished up some audition pieces. My voice was changing and was a problem to some members of 'The Priests.' They had known me as a rebellious teenager with a northern accent and now, not only was I a Christian but, my voice had changed. To them, it was difficult to grasp. I became embarrassed at times and made a diversion if I saw any of them, apart from Paul and another friend. They were fine with me.

There was still a lot of work to do. Somehow I felt I was missing something regarding training. Jean-Pierre had, by this time, moved into the top of an old Victorian House. Next door was a young lady called Angela. She would occasionally meet up to chat with Jean-Pierre and the other members of the household. Jean-Pierre told me once that he was not sure of the voice that I had and assumed that I had put it on. He soon realised that this was for real. If anyone had noticed a change it was Jean-Pierre, after all, we had spent most of our lives together as friends and he knew what I was like at school, as well as knowing all about the drugs, crime and alcohol, etc. I felt that I was ready to audition at another drama school and, whilst walking through Liverpool, Richmond Drama School came to me. It had been embedded in my subconscious from somewhere, maybe word of mouth. I left a message on the answer phone for the director David Whitworth, who was an actor, enjoyed Shakespeare and had won international awards for directing them. I filled in the application form and was offered an audition. Richard, by now a very good friend, kindly let me, once again, stay at his house.

On the day of the audition, Ian Sparks (a friend from SCM) had joined us. He, himself, knew what the business was like. He had struggled, but finally God was richly blessing him. Ian was a fantastic Roy Orbison look-a-like and singer. We walked around Richmond for a while and I remember Richard saying, 'You will be here soon.'

'If only that was true,' I said to myself. As I walked through the doors into the studio I saw David Whitworth. He reminded me of Peter O'Toole with his mannerisms and voice. He was pleasant but firm with regards to acting. I walked out to the front and performed to the best of my ability. God is good because, in the past, you generally have to wait for a letter to tell you if you have been accepted or not. David looked at me and said, 'I would love to have you as a student.' This was great. He had put me out my misery.

I was still doubtful and waited impatiently for confirmation whilst back at my mum and dad's house in Birkenhead. It was not long before the confirmation letter arrived. It was true. I was finally going to a drama school where plays were performed: Richmond Drama School would perform a least ten plays a year and also incorporated dance, drama, singing, world theatre, and Shakespeare classes (a favorite of mine). It would also include keeping fit and healthy. Something David Whitworth believed in.

As with everything related to studying, finances were a problem in my life. How was I going to pay and live? This would take a miracle, but God had a plan. I remember Paul Epton saying to me when he found out, 'You will get a house.' It was difficult to believe. I told Jean-Pierre and had a divine appointment with Angela, who just so happened to be good at fundraising and knew about writing. We spent time with each other and I enjoyed our friendship. However, I became very stressed because I still had no money or accommodation.

I started to write to churches in Richmond and the

surrounding areas. Meanwhile Angela had got me an interview on BBC Radio Merseyside and features in three newspapers. I had some response from the articles but nothing financial. Whilst in my parent's house, I received a strange phone call from a gentleman. He wanted to help and asked if I could visit him. I agreed but was rather suspicious and, when meeting him, there was a sense of unease about him. He chatted and said that he wanted to start his own drama school in the area. He was very adamant about this. Anyway, I left him and a few days later received another phone call, this time from David Whitworth. He was concerned for me. 'Are you not coming to train here?' he asked

'I definitely am,' I replied.

Apparently, the gentleman I had chatted to phoned David Whitworth from Richmond Drama School conveying the story that I was setting up my own drama school. This was not true, so I mentioned it to the newspapers and Stuart Melling. Nothing ever came of it.

There was still the issue of fees and I was introduced to Angela's mum and step-dad. They had listened to the interview I did on BBC Radio Merseyside with Linda McDermott. They wanted to help and agreed to pay the first term. God had come through. I then received a letter from a Pastor at Teddington Baptist Church with news that a Mrs. Dora Willis had a room and I could lodge with her. At last I started to feel relieved and less stressed. It was time for another Journey. Richmond Drama School would be tough, hard work, but fun. I prayed to God that this time I would never have a day off and complete the full time course. I decided to go and visit Tony Holland at his Christian Gym in Birkenhead. Tony, to those who don't remember, had won *Opportunity Knocks* with his wonderful dancing muscles. Tony, himself, has a story to tell and has been on many TV programmes. His gym was well-equipped. He knew his stuff and was very knowledgeable. His gentleness shone as well as always having time to listen, but if he needed to be firm he would be. Although a Christian gym, it was open to non- Christians. He was honest about his faith, but didn't impose Christianity on his members. He was very helpful. It was interesting to see these body-builders respect Tony and his Christianity. I would visit Tony on many occasions, not only to workout but for advice and general chat. On this occasion I wanted to talk to him about food and what would be best to help me through drama school.

CHAPTER 17

Acorn and – Now - Oak Tree of Acting

'Christians in Entertainment' were praying for me and I had settled into my new home at Dora Willis'. She was rather old, but vibrant, and had one daughter living with her. Richmond Drama School was a bus ride away in the lovely town of Richmond. One by one the students arrived. It was a good mix of actors from different countries as well. I noticed a good looking chap come in. He sat next to me and his name was Theo van Dort. We really got on together. David Whitworth introduced his wife called Jane (she had trained at RADA) and Clare who was the voice teacher. Tabby was the fitness teacher and Urshele was the Singing teacher. Other teachers also came in from time to time.

Jane, over the next few months, worked with us on acting and I learnt so much. We were asked to keep a diary, which I still have. Clare would frighten the living daylights out of me. I was terrified of her criticising my voice, but underneath that firmness she was a real gentle person. David taught Shakespeare and directed. Tabby worked us really hard and got us into shape. As actors, we got to the point of being able to do an hour of song and dance without being tired.

It was a full-time drama course and we never stopped performing. David and Jane covered Chekhov, Shakespeare, Homer and many more. The reviews in the newspapers were very good and what a delight it was to see my name mentioned so many times. Some of what I had learned at method school came in handy at times. Jane had cast me as Antinous from *The Odyssey* and I really wanted to get into character. On this particular night it was raining and the wind was strong. In the story there is a scene on a boat with a storm, so I opened the window and recited my lines. It was great and I felt the atmosphere of how the lines should be said. I was taught to remember the experience and recall it on the day of performance.

Katherine Connolly, David Noble and Joe Early also helped in the sense that they became good friends who I could trust if I needed to talk. The closest out of all the women was Davina; she was like a sister to me and I enjoyed our talks. I had my first stage kiss with her, which was rather embarrassing. There were times when I didn't eat properly because of money and Theo was like a brother to me during these times. He provided money and, although not a Christian, he was kind and thoughtful to me. However, I didn't have the money to pay for my last term at drama school and asked Sally from 'Christians in Entertainment 'if she would pray for me. In my room, one night, the phone rang. It was a Mr. Brighton (someone from a media group who had been passed my name with regards to praying for me from Christians in Entertainment). He said that he had been praying for me. I shared my dilemma and he asked me where I would be that night. I was actually going to cycle to my friend Richard's house in Warlingham. Mr. Brighton wanted to help me with money and I remember him saying, 'Just praise God.'

'How can I praise God? Here I am with no food and no fees," I said to myself. Anyway, that night, in the rain, I cycled and met up with Richard. What happened next was a blessing. Richard told me that a gentleman had arrived at his door with a box of food and an envelope full of money. It had been Mr. John Brighton, who also paid my last term's fees. I am truly grateful for his generosity. An answer to prayer he certainly became. I have never met him but would love to one day to thank him for his kindness. Who knows, one day, in London, maybe I may come across him.

Angela, meanwhile, also had good news. She had secured over four thousand pounds to help pay for the fees at drama school. After paying back Mr. Brighton I was left with a nice sum of money. Richmond Drama School was a success. At this time my voice felt natural and I had learned so much about acting. I had been professionally trained. All I needed was an Equity card, work and a wife.

CHAPTER 18

RADA: To Be or Not To Be?

I had been single for such a long time and, as a Christian, could not understand why God had not blessed me with a wife. I was 29 and had been praying for many years. It had been difficult, not just sexually but learning about relationships. God was changing me and helping me to mature and understand that there was more to a relationship than just lust. Maybe I would remain single for the rest of my life, I thought. Although Angela had been a good, supportive friend, I felt that this was only ever meant to be a friendship.

My mum and dad had gone on holiday leaving me to look after the house in Birkenhead. Unfortunately, I had had a panic attack and became very anxious again, as I felt empty and did not know what to do with my life. After all, I had been away at drama school for a year and now, here, I didn't know what to do with my life. I had nothing to do. I didn't want to stay at home and arranged to spend time with Vincent and Donna, who had now moved to Nantwich. He was training at a bible school (something I tried but hated when I was at SCM). In two weeks I had lost a stone in weight. It was a difficult time. Eating food was very difficult and when my mum and dad returned they could tell that there was something wrong with me. I was bold and told them that I had not eaten. 'I need to put weight on,' I said to my mum. The next few weeks were a struggle. People were saying things in front of me about my weight. I found it difficult to sleep. One lady whispered to my mum, 'He's very skinny.' That was the last straw, I had to do something. I remember saying to myself, 'You will put weight on.' I felt God's hand upon me and started with chocolate biscuits and milk. Nearly every night I would go to the shop and buy chocolate biscuits, rush up to my room and scoff them. Slowly, the weight came on. I was still stressed and anxious about my life and being an actor, because I didn't know what the future held, but I knew that I needed to trust God. He had provided financially and I needed to trust him in other areas of my life too.

It was a sunny day and I sat reading The Stage newspaper, which I enjoyed reading. Suddenly I noticed that RADA were offering courses in Shakespeare and method acting (subject to your CV). This was it! I got my dad to send a cheque for the fees and a CV. God was good. The moment had arrived and there on the doorstep was a white envelope with the famous RADA name written on it in red. I opened the letter and saw the magic words, 'We have pleasure in inviting you to RADA.' Yes! At last I was going to RADA to study. I had enjoyed Shakespeare and had spent years reading about practical aspects of acting Shakespeare. So it wasn't three years. 'Who cares!' I said. It was still RADA and I would learn something.

I spoke to Sally Goring and she was delighted. She prayed for accommodation and God didn't let me down. Liz and Arthur Wynyard from Kingston upon Thames had contacted me regarding a poster that they had seen in their church about my wanting accommodation. At first it didn't go to plan. I hadn't got a job and Liz didn't get back to me regarding my lodging with them. However, after praying, I felt that I should contact them again. This time Liz said, 'Yes, and don't worry about the rent, God will provide.' God did provide.

As I walked down Gower Street, London, I could feel the excitement in me. It was time. There I was, finally walking through the famous RADA doors and it wasn't an audition, but training. The teachers were great. I learned how to perform Shakespeare's language and another technique where you retain energy (which comes from improvisation) and transfer it to the scene or character situations. Method acting was interesting as well and over all a valuable experience.

I could have done more courses, but money was an issue. While I was staying at Liz and Arthur's I had an opportunity to audition for a Shakespeare Company. The director asked if I was available to join his Company that very month if I was successful. I said, 'Yes,' but as the weeks went by I realised that the director had probably chosen another actor. I remember a Christian saying to me, 'Ask God. He is your Dad.' Taking his advice, I did ask God about the possibility of one day becoming a member of a Shakespeare Company, then forgot all about it. Many months later I received a phone call from the Shakespeare Company. They wanted me to join them and play Quince and Egeus from *A Midsummer Night's Dream*. I said yes. This was another ambition of mine - to join a Shakespeare Company. Around this time Liz had got me a job in Iceland Food Stores. It was all right, but I wanted to be an actor not stuck behind a counter. I allowed my temper to get the better of me when I witnessed a member of staff bullying another. Well, I ran at him but he backed away. I decided to leave the job because I hated injustice. It was the wrong thing to do, but Liz encouraged me to complain as it wasn't right to leave a job because of this incident. A few days later I found myself working again at Iceland. The situation had been dealt with. I started to learn from Liz how important it was to earn a living, not to just exist, and it was a form of discipline that was good for me.

Rehearsals were long with the Shakespeare Youth Company. Our director was strict and had been working with Stephen Berkoff. There were only two weeks to rehearse. At last we performed and we were very successful. I was now being paid for being an actor.

However, the work dried up and it was time to leave Liz and Arthur's after a year. This would be the last training that I would do in London. I had learned so much about myself and life skills including taking responsibility for oneself.

CHAPTER 19

An Actor Begins

I had come a long way in life. God had taken someone from the streets; a criminal, involved in gang warfare, drugs, gambling, alcohol and sexual abuse, and changed me. I had a long way to go, but a change had taken place. God reversed the situation so rather than fighting with authorities I was working with them. Police had become colleagues, teachers had become friends and I had a heart for people like never before. The drinking had stopped, which was my personal choice and gambling was not an addiction any more. I was a gentleman; able to converse with most people on the social ladder. Ron had played his part, so had Stuart Melling and I decided to use my voice and train in BBC commercial broadcasting. I even had my own arts show, but this was not the end; it was merely the beginning of something new.

I was now in my thirties and sometimes had to be reminded that I was still young. Training helped me to get something that I had wanted for many years, which was an Equity card. It was so exciting. I couldn't stop looking at it. Would this be the key to a successful career? Well, as any actor knows, only a small percentage of actors are working at any one time, but guess what? It didn't stop me.

God had a wonderful idea: I needed to share what he had done for me. Over the next few years I found myself in Christian newspapers, on the front covers of magazines, being interviewed on Christian radios stations and TV chat shows and talking openly about my life. I met up again with Nigel Goodwin and Carrie and David Grant in London when they were talking about their careers at an arts meeting. It was a lovely moment and they were a blessing to me. Carrie and David are now very successful in TV-land and Nigel Goodwin has chatted to me and encouraged me to move forward. I started running the Art Centre Group in Merseyside and I thank God for Sally Goring for her support and encouragement. As this chapter says, 'It's an actor's life.'

With my Equity card and Jean-Pierre's help with photographs, I was ready for the market place. Ron Gittins was proud of me, but I needed to continue. The training was behind me and now it was time to break into TV and Film. Being an actor was very stressful and I had to put up with the constant nagging to get a real job from some people around me. Some Christians had said that if you are not working then maybe it's not God's will. This was a misunderstanding about the arts and generally came from concerned Christian views. It wasn't long before my sister approached me with some good news about work. Suzanne had seen an advertisement in a local newspaper asking for local actors to audition for a feature film. I was excited and took a chance by sending my CV off to the director, Douglas Byrne. After a few days I received a phone call from Douglas asking if I would like to meet up with him. I agreed and decided to have a drink with him next to Beatties. Douglas was pleasant and had a soft approach. He explained to me that it was going to be a thriller, but would not be scripted. He was going to use improvisation. After our drink, he offered me the part of a medical student, which fitted in well with the way that I spoke. *Fear*, was the title and it was filmed over a few weeks around various locations in Wirral. I had a great time and befriended all of the actors. Carl Wharton and Pete Legg were part of the cast and, to this day, we occasionally see or speak to each other. Carl has been inspirational regarding some of the teaching projects that I have done. *Fear* was about a group of students and teachers who decided to have a beach party. However, things don't go according to plan and my character is blamed. The film was premiered at the town hall on a large screen. *Fear* was not to everyone's taste, but it did make it onto video.

One Sunday morning, after hearing from a friend, called Mike

Ryan, that BBC Radio Merseyside had a programme on Sunday mornings which was predominately Christian, I asked if I could use his phone and contacted Wayne Clarke, a minister and presenter on the show. We had a long chat and he asked if I could meet up with him. It was voluntary and not paid. Experience of working on BBC Radio was enough and I know it was not acting, but I did train in Radio and here was an opportunity to put it into practice. Wayne Clarke had appeared on University Challenge many years before. He had a team of committed volunteers who helped with reading the news, interviews and reviews of the newspapers. I arrived at Radio Merseyside and was reminded of the last time that I was there. First, at the age of eight, with Billy Butler and on that specific day I was wearing shorts and sang a song in the large studio. The second time was with Linda McDermott. She had interviewed me about getting money for Richmond Drama School. Her parting words were, 'Maybe we will see you in five years with a Shakespeare Company.' BBC Radio Merseyside was then in Paradise Street. I was greeted by Wayne and he sat down with me. I shared my testimony with him and mentioned that I was the area contact for The Arts Centre Group. He needed to fill a slot for his Sunday Show and wanted to interview me. This was great, another opportunity to share my life and market myself as an actor. After the interview he asked me to join the team and read the news live on Sundays. I agreed and spent the next few years doing many radio features for Wayne.

CHAPTER 20

I Do

The year was 2002 and I had been involved in *Hollyoaks* playing a bouncer, but I was lonely and spoke many times with Sally from 'Christians in Entertainment.' I remember her telling me that there may be someone around the corner.

Now, I had been asked by Norman Polden (a good Christian friend and like a spiritual father to me) to interview some special guests at God in the Park. I had interviewed some face painters from Oasis Church Center and decided that I would visit the church the next day to worship and put up some drama posters for young people. The event and interviews were for Flame Christian Radio on Wirral. Cannon and Ball (already Christians) were on that week, so I arranged to interview them. It was a short chat but fun and rewarding; I had what I needed. Bobby took time to chat to me regarding being a Christian and working as an actor. He was encouraging. As mentioned, a few Christians didn't look favorably upon Christians working in secular entertainment. However, God had a plan and I felt that I was in the right job.

The next day I visited Oasis Church to worship God and to look for the special person that I believed God had for me. I arrived at Oasis Church, in Wallasey, dressed in a suit and long Cromby jacket. During the service a beautiful lady came up to the platform and started to share her testimony. She was petite and had blonde hair. I listened as she painfully described and revealed her past. She had been divorced because of her husband's adultery and had been left with a child who was now two and a half years old. I remember telling God that I would love to meet her, then I misunderstood something that she had said and assumed that she had now found a new man because she had described how God had transformed her. I gave up hope of meeting her and went home. About four months later I received an email from New Day Introductions (a Christian dating agency). It described details of a lady called Pauline and I decided to phone her. I was reluctant at first, not least because she was 5ft 3in tall and I always wanted someone a lot taller. However, as shy as I was, I plucked up the courage to phone her. Thank God it was an answer machine. I left a message. Late that night the phone rang and it was Pauline returning my call. I was nervous but continued to chat. At the end of the conversation I asked her to meet up for a coffee (or, in my case, coke). She then told me that she was attending Oasis and, as she described herself, it suddenly dawned on me that it was the same lady who was sharing her testimony four months before. I was excited because I knew that this wasn't going to be a blind date and she was beautiful. I told her that I knew who she was and she was surprised and quite shocked that I had heard her testimony. I knew all about her situation and circumstances.

The day had arrived for us to meet. We had arranged to meet at St. Werburgh's clock next to Beatties in Birkenhead. The only problem was that I had forgotten how tall she was and, as I stood next to a bench, was surprised by how many blonde girls came towards me. The minutes rolled by and I was now becoming anxious that I had missed her. I thought that she might be sitting in the coffee place waiting for me, but then, coming towards me, was this beautiful, petite lady with blonde hair.

'Hello,' I said, but didn't kiss her. I was far too shy for that. We went for a drink in the café nearby and started to talk. I was excited and words wouldn't stop coming out, but inside I was very nervous. To our astonishment we had so much in common. In the beginning of this book I mentioned that there was a secret over the road from Abacus Taxis in Rock Ferry. It turned out that Pauline had grown up next to the library, opposite my home. Her brother used to play with my sister and brother. As we talked we also realised that, sixteen years earlier, we had been in the same drama group (The Carlton Players: a very professional group who I really enjoyed working with). I was performing in a play called 'Semi-detached,' at the 'Little Theatre' and Pauline was doing 'A Man for All Seasons' and 'Change of Air.' This was also where, during my time performing 'Semi-Detached,' I met my old head master, Mr. Powell, who played my boss. It was no coincidence that we had been brought together.

After a few dates I still did not pluck up the courage to show any sign of affection towards her. I did not really know how to date as a Christian and worried that I would do the wrong thing. So I thought that I would ring her and tell her that I did not want to meet up again. Pauline sensed that something was strange and, because of her past, was happy to take things slowly anyway. When I phoned her she thought that maybe God has someone else in mind for her. She then realised that I was afraid to show affection. She said, 'Never mind that things didn't work out for us, but if you meet someone you like try and show them some affection.'

Pauline was convinced that she would never hear from me again, but hoped that she could help me out of my shyness. She felt sorry for me, as my shyness was crippling me. This was maybe because I did not grow up a Christian and at the age of nineteen, when I gave my life to Christ, I just did not understand the rules of engagement in close relationships. I so wanted a relationship that was right with God. I did not want sex before marriage and believed that it should be with the person that God had chosen for me. Non-Christians (those that I had grown up with) would have been surprised and may not have understood. However, God had other plans and Pauline was on my mind a lot over the next few weeks, until one evening I realised that maybe God wanted me to have a relationship with Pauline. I plucked up the courage to phone her and explained my fears. Pauline knew about this, as she had sensed it. After a chat on the phone I asked if we could start afresh and arranged to meet in Chester. From that moment on Pauline and I began to grow in our relationship.

Three months later, I asked Vincent and Donna if I should ask Pauline to marry me. Donna had no hesitation and then said yes. She was eager to meet her as I had told Donna and Vincent all about her. Donna was intrigued about the woman who had captured my heart, as it had been so difficult to set up.

It was a late evening and, as we sat on the settee, I proposed to her and to my joy, she said yes.

All of my life I had been waiting for this moment. It was exciting and she rang me the next morning to see whether it was true. Did I really ask her? Yes I did. We worked hard to arrange the wedding, wanting to get that part out of the way (we both knew what our families were like at interfering with wedding plans).

When I told my mum and dad and the rest of the family I don't think that they believed me. It had been so long and I was a committed bachelor to them.

Pauline surprised me and chose my birthday as our wedding day and Stratford upon Avon for our honeymoon. God was with us and many financial miracles happened. Wayne Clarke agreed to marry us and I chose Jean-Pierre as my best man. Richard Ford was going to read for me. I also invited Michelle, who was a friend in Croydon and someone that I could chat to. Pauline had her friends as well. The big day arrived at Oasis church and Tony and Debbie Tasack had worked diligently to decorate the hall like a fairytale. It was lovely.

The rehearsal was funny because things went wrong. Christopher, Pauline's son and now mine, ran at Wayne Clarke with plastic screwdrivers into his private parts. Pauline and I could not stop laughing from embarrassment, but Wayne didn't mind as he was a professional.

On the day, it was magical and Pauline looked wonderful. This was the moment; the time when we became one with each other; the place where both of us looked at each other and said, 'I Do.'

CHAPTER 21

An Actor's Life

Pauline and I were now married and I was a step-dad. Stratford upon Avon was special for both of us and, after seeing the RSC performance of *Richard the Third*, I wanted to work even more, not only as an actor, but, one day, with the RSC. At that moment this was just another one of my ambitions.

I had the opportunity, one day, to be in the right place at the right time. Up to this point I didn't have an agent but continued doing bits and pieces. I had heard that Equity had a branch in Liverpool and, one night, after much thought, encouragement and persuasion from Pauline, I decided to go with her. I arrived at my first Equity meeting. Most people, if not all, on that night, were a lot older than I was. Ron Harrison was the chair person; he was warm, humorous and good fun. Ron was a retired headmaster and had entered the profession later on in life when he was sixty two. He had already been in many drama's such as *In the Name of the Father; Let Him Have It* and a nice character part in *Peter's Kay Phoenix Nights*. Joe was also there that night. He had dark hair and olive skin and wore a flying jacket and white scarf. He introduced himself to me. Looking back he reminded me of the scrounger in *The Great Escape*. He was in the know and had already built up a rapport with certain agencies. Joe was a genuine chap and eager to help a young actor like myself. Then there was Kevin McMahon who was an actor, writer and director. He knew a lot about the business and was very much in the know with certain people. Kevin was enthusiastic about learning about film and protective of Equity members. After the meetings we would retire to The Everyman bar and network. Kevin had enrolled on a film course and suggested that we should do the same. What did we have to lose? We found out that a film festival was being launched in Liverpool and there was an opportunity to make a three to four minute film. In the class, we got the working titles by drawing names out of a hat. Our's was called 'Hello.' For the next few weeks we filmed and worked with Joe's idea. It was a thriller about spies. I played Oxford. Jean-Pierre documented the experiences with photographs and also designed the DVD cover. He had also designed the cover for *Fear* a few years before. The end result was not bad and won best stylish short film. Ron Harrison took me under his wing and, as a young actor, his knowledge was very valuable. It was not long before the jobs started coming my way. I was offered a part in *Titanic: Birth of a Legend*. It was to play an Irish protestant worker. It was a non-speaking part, but I was in it a lot. I remember arriving very early at Cammell Lairds Ship yard and seeing the huge set looking like 1912. The set designers had also built a large landing stage and a replica section of the Titanic. The costumes were great. I was dressed in ninetieth century clothes with a cap. It was great fun and filming, for me, lasted around four weeks. What a joy when it was shown. I was on national TV. People would approach me and tell me they had seen me. I finally got an agent and, one afternoon, she phoned me and told me that she was putting me forward for a lawyer part. BBC 1 *Real Story* was doing a drama documentary about satanic abuse in Rockdale in 1991. I auditioned for it and did some research beforehand, so as an actor I was prepared. With a camera in front of us we began to improvise. It was great fun and the casting people were impressed. As with all auditions, you can never tell what the panel is thinking, but Pauline was very positive and we prayed for many days. Days later, I remember my mobile vibrating. It was my agent calling to tell me that I had got the part of the lawyer. This was fantastic - my first major speaking part on TV, or at least I thought. On my arrival I noticed someone I knew walking towards me. It was a friend from *Fear* - Carl Wharton. Carl and I talked a lot that day about Shakespeare and running drama workshops. We spent an entire day filming and the crew filmed in a real courtroom.

One of the things that I did as an actor was to contact the local newspapers. I had so much coming out on TV around the same time. At this time I realised that I needed to polish up and choose more audition pieces. You never know when they would be needed. I chose Margaret Parsons of Arkney School of Speech and Drama. She had been in *Emmerdale*. Margaret was tall and elegant with a rich voice. Her studios were very high class. On her wall were newspaper cuttings and actors photographs. She was very good and supportive. Our training was professional and it was like being back at drama school. Margaret taught me so much, building up my confidence. I hope that Margaret and I will work together again some day. It was also a desire of mine to give back some of the things that I had learnt at drama school to young people, so I enrolled on two courses that helped me to obtain relevant training as a drama practitioner. I am grateful for Hope Street Limited, Liverpool and St. Helen's College for their support and faith in me and culminating in my receiving a teaching certificate and a certificate for training as a workshop leader.

At home, I received a phone call from a journalist wanting to interview me about my acting. The article was good and got me noticed. Unfortunately, when *Real Story* was shown all of the actor's speaking parts, apart from the judge, had been cut. This was due to running time, but I was still seen as the lawyer a few times in the programme. I give thanks to God for that.

As a family we have now found a good spiritual home near our home. As an actor I am now in the spotlight and have done many things in TV, theatre and radio. My life has been an adventure but thanks to ACG and 'Christians in Entertainment' I was able to continue. Being an actor and a Christian is not easy but God needs people in all sorts of jobs. Acting is a market place and a place where we meet people from all walks of life. It's an opportunity to play and identify with other people's lives;

fictional or real. I am still learning and God is still guiding me in my life. In the Bible we read in Paul's letters to the Corinthians that God talks about comforting us in our problems so that we can comfort other people. The devil tried to destroy my life with drugs, sexual abuse, crime, and alcohol, but God is rebuilding me with faith, love and acceptance. When I look at my difficult and often traumatic background, I am grateful to God and all those who have been an encouragement and help to me. Who would have thought that someone with a speech impediment, all those years ago, would appear regularly on BBC radio; someone who had deprived himself of an education would be teaching in theatre schools (including Wirral Academy of Performing Arts). God took me from the street to the stage and I have recently been back (after ten years) on the Linda McDermott Late Night Show, sharing my story live on BBC Radio Merseyside. I have also had the opportunity of being in two pantomimes with the Chrysanthemums Pantomime Society (whose home has been the Floral Pavilion for many years). I performed in *Jack and the beanstalk* playing the Giant, and the Demon wolf in *Babes in the wood*. With my knowledge and training, both in acting and spirituality, I now desire to serve Christ in the entertainment industries.

BOOKS

O is a symbol of the world, of oneness and unity. In different cultures it also means the "eye," symbolizing knowledge and insight. We aim to publish books that are accessible, constructive and that challenge accepted opinion, both that of academia and the "moral majority."

Our books are available in all good English language bookstores worldwide. If you don't see the book on the shelves ask the bookstore to order it for you, quoting the ISBN number and title. Alternatively you can order online (all major online retail sites carry our titles) or contact the distributor in the relevant country, listed on the copyright page.

See our website www.o-books.net for a full list of over 500 titles, growing by 100 a year.

And tune in to myspiritradio.com for our book review radio show, hosted by June-Elleni Laine, where you can listen to the authors discussing their books.

mySpiRitRaòio